W9-BRA-120

LET the MEATBALLS REST

and

Other Stories About Food and Culture

Arts and Traditions of the Table

ARTS AND TRADITIONS OF THE TABLE
PERSPECTIVES ON CULINARY HISTORY

ALBERT SONNENFELD, SERIES EDITOR

Salt: Grain of Life, Pierre Laszlo, translated by Mary Beth Mader

Culture of the Fork, Giovanni Rebora, translated by Albert Sonnenfeld

French Gastronomy: The History and Geography of a Passion,
Jean-Robert Pitte, translated by Jody Gladding

Pasta: The Story of a Universal Food,
Silvano Serventi and Françoise Sabban, translated by Antony Shugar

Slow Food: The Case for Taste, Carlo Petrini, translated by William McCuaig

Italian Cuisine: A Cultural History,
Alberto Capatti and Massimo Montanari, translated by Áine O'Healy

British Food: An Extraordinary Thousand Years of History, Colin Spencer

A Revolution in Eating: How the Quest for Food Shaped America,
James E. McWilliams

Sacred Cow, Mad Cow: A History of Food Fears, Madeleine Ferrières,
translated by Jody Gladding

Molecular Gastronomy: Exploring the Science of Flavor,
Hervé This, translated by M. B. DeBevoise

Food Is Culture, Massimo Montanari, translated by Albert Sonnenfeld

Kitchen Mysteries: Revealing the Science of Cooking,
Hervé This, translated by Jody Gladding

Hog and Hominy: Soul Food from Africa to America, Frederick Douglass Opie

Gastropolis: Food and New York City,
edited by Annie Hauck-Lawson and Jonathan Deutsch

Building a Meal: From Molecular Gastronomy to Culinary Constructivism,
Hervé This, translated by M. B. DeBevoise

Eating History: Thirty Turning Points in the Making of American Cuisine,
Andrew F. Smith

The Science of the Oven, Hervé This, translated by Jody Gladding

Pomodoro! A History of the Tomato in Italy, David Gentilcore

Cheese, Pears, and History in a Proverb, Massimo Montanari,
translated by Beth Archer Brombert

Food and Faith in Christian Culture, edited by Ken Albals and Trudy Eden

The Kitchen as Laboratory: Reflections on the Science of Food and Cooking, edited by
César Vega, Job Ubbink, and Erik van der Linden

LET the MEATBALLS REST and Other Stories About Food and Culture

MASSIMO MONTANARI

TRANSLATED BY BETH ARCHER BROMBERT

COLUMBIA UNIVERSITY PRESS
NEW YORK

Columbia University Press
Publishers Since 1893
New York   Chichester, West Sussex

Copyright © 2009 Gius. Laterza & Figli.
Published by agreement with Marco Vigevani Agenzia Letteraria.
Translation copyright © 2012 Columbia University Press
All rights reserved
The translation of the work has been funded by SEPS
Segretariato Europeo per le Pubblicazioni Scientifiche

Via Val d'Aposa 7
40123 Bologna, Italy
seps@seps.it—www.seps.it

Library of Congress Cataloging-in-Publication Data
Montanari, Massimo, 1949–
[Riposo della polpetta e altre storie intorno al cibo. English]
Let the meatballs rest, and other stories about food and culture /
Massimo Montanari ; translated by Beth Archer Brombert
pages cm
Includes index.
ISBN 978-0-231-15732-2 (cloth : alk. paper)
ISBN 978-0-231-52788-0 (ebook)
1. Cooking—History. 2. Cooking—Philosophy. 3. Food habits—History.
4. Food habits—Philosophy. I. Title.

TX645.M6613   2012
641.5—dc23   2012021330

∞

Columbia University Press books are printed
on permanent and durable acid-free paper.

This book is printed on paper with recycled content.
Printed in the United States of America

Designed by Julia Kushnirsky

c 10 9 8 7 6 5 4 3 2 1

References to Internet Web sites (URLs) were accurate at the time
of writing. Neither the author nor Columbia University Press
is responsible for URLs that may have expired or changed
since the manuscript was prepared.

CONTENTS

Introduction   ix

1. Things and Ideas   1

Being and eating / The invention of bread / Our daily bread / Festive bread / Bread unites or divides? / Divide meat, share soup / Form and substance (discussion around a plate of pasta)

2. The Status of Foods   12

Esau's lentils, or how farmers defeated hunters / Flour from spelt / "Inferior" grains? / Liquid bread: from ale to beer / The stench of garlic / The king's peas (and the peasant's too) / The potato, from emergency food to culinary specialty / The eggplant, food of plebeians or Jews / The bread tree / The peaches of Messer Lippo / Five hundred pears / To die for a melon / Strawberries in November / Watermelons and cucumbers / Sweet as a fig

3. Adventures in Cooking   38

From raw to cooked (and back) / The prefect recipe / Cappelletti and tortellini: the retro-taste of history / Macaroni, or is it gnocchi? / The patient took some broth / The invention of fried potatoes / Among the thousand ways to prepare eggs / Fritters / Don't flip the frittata / Sausages / Pink pigs, black pigs / Liberating vegetarian cooking / Dressing a salad / The blender and the mortar /

Mediterranean "fusion" / Home cooking: when variation is the rule / Cooking is home

4. The Gastronomy of Hunger 65

Nameless plants / Field herbs / Forgotten fruits, or rediscovered? / The struggle against time / Diversity as a resource / Bread of earth / The right to pleasure / Rivers of milk and giant tomatoes

5. Flavors 78

Flavor and knowledge / How many flavors are there? / A longing for sweet / Sweet and/or salty / Bitter to the taste / When sour was fashionable / The taste for spices (and hot pepper) / The taste of smoke / How chocolate became sweet / The taste of canned foods

6. Pleasure and Health 94

"What tastes good is good for you" / The law of opposites, between kitchen and pharmacy / Watermelon, salt and pepper / Monthly diets / The language of the navel / Fat, meaning meat / "Indigestion does not bother peasants" / The lightness of the monk / When pleasure frightens / Monastic gastronomy / Philosophizing gluttony

7. The Beautiful and the Good 112

The making of colors / White or red? / Carrot red / Culinary artifices / Compositions and compotes / *Confetti* (sugarcoated almonds, spices, etc.) / Beauty is not a superfluous benefit

8. Convivial Rituals 123

The call of the wild (around the barbecue) / A masculine ritual / Rucola in the White House / Christmas dinner / A hundred cappelletti / Carnival and Lent / Lenten diet, gastronomic discoveries / Easter eggs / Breakfast / When snacking kills the snack / Silence, we're eating / Eating on the highway / Fast food and conviviality

9. Table Practices and Manners 143

The fork and the hands / The missing cutlery / The pot on the table / First or second? / The wheel of food / To pour, to mix: when wine was made by the Imbider / The ancient art of pairing wine with food / How to taste wine (without making an ass of oneself) / Cold drinks

10. "Identity" Declined in the Plural   157

Spaghetti with tomato sauce, or the other in us / Pasta and the Italians: a single and multiple identity / Macaroni-eaters / Four pies / One product, one city: Bologna and mortadella / Pellegrino Artusi: Italian identity in the world / Polenta and couscous (with an unexpected variant) / Is McDonald's compatible with local identities?

Index   171

INTRODUCTION

We were making meatballs in the kitchen one evening: boiled beef, cooked cardoons, parmesan, bread crumbs, two eggs, salt, pepper. Once the mixture was done, we shaped the meatballs and arranged them neatly on a plate. At that point, Marina advised: "Now, before cooking them, let us leave them to rest for a few hours. That way they firm up and get thoroughly blended."

It occurred to me that letting meatballs rest is much like what happens in our minds when we work out an idea. Ideas are the result of experiences, encounters, reflections, suggestions: many "ingredients" that come together and then turn into a new thought. Before that can happen, it is useful to let those ingredients rest, to give them time to settle, to become blended, to firm up. The resting of meatballs is like the resting of thoughts: After a while, they turn out better.

The kitchen is not just the place where survival and pleasure are planned. It is also an ideal place for training the mind. To observe the processes of cooking, the transformation of raw materials subjected to the heat of the stove, the incontrovertible rules of suitability (some things go well together, others do not), the order and sequence of actions (done in a particular order and a particular rhythm can produce excellent results, done differently can cause disasters, as when a mayonnaise curdles), can allow us to contemplate the rules that govern daily life, the things that happen around us each day, our relationship with the world, with others, with ourselves. Cooking is not an inferior activity; it stimulates the intelligence. This view is also held by a famous lady of the seventeenth century, Sister Juana Inès de la Cruz, the major poet of the Mexican Baroque. In her proud affirmation of the role of women (which caused her no small amount of derision in the macho society of the time), she defended the intellectual dimension of preparing food, comparing it to philosophical reflection and even declaring its superiority. "What can I tell you," wrote Sister Juana, "about the secrets of nature that I discovered while I was cooking? I see an egg that solidifies as it fries in butter or oil, and on the contrary separates in syrup; I see that for sugar to remain free-flowing it is enough to add a tiny amount of water in which a quince or some other acidy fruit has been placed; I see that the yolk and the white of the same egg are such contrary entities that with sugar they can be whipped but never together." These observations are far more profound than they would seem at first glance, so that, Sister Juana concludes provocatively, "One can easily philosophize while preparing dinner. I maintain that Aristotle would have written much more had he cooked."

In the following pages I have collected a hundred short pieces that appeared during the past few years in *Consumatori*, the monthly magazine of the Coop Adriatica, and in the Sunday pages of the newspaper *La Repubblica*. I thank the directors of both publications for allowing me to reprint these articles, to which I have added a few small pieces that were published elsewhere. Small, but I hope not without interest, because I have always held the conviction that important topics can also be treated lightly, starting from "simple" reflections on facts, things, words, that cross our path and that, despite their seeming banality, contain meaningful fragments about our history and express important aspects of our culture.

An idea of which I am particularly fond, which inspires my scholarly work and which I try to communicate even in the most nonacademic circles, is that the practices of cooking (in its broadest sense, everything that has to do with food: modes of preparation, techniques of transformation, modalities of consumption, rituals of conviviality) not only constitute a sizable segment of the cultural patrimony of a society, but in many cases reveal fundamental mechanisms of our material and intellectual behavior. Cooking can thus be regarded as a metaphor for life—unless we recognize that life itself is a metaphor for cooking.

LET the MEATBALLS REST

and

Other Stories About Food and Culture

ONE

Things and Ideas

Being and eating

A German philosopher of the nineteenth century, Ludwig Feuerbach, wrote a line destined for great fame, which we often quote: "Man is what he eats." What he meant is that a man's identity does not depend on abstractions but coincides with his corporality, and thus on the food that day after day enters his body, enabling him to live and function. Feuerbach expressed a radically materialistic idea of man and the world, reducing all reality, be they things or ideas, to their concrete dimension.

Feuerbach naturally wrote in German, and in German this famous line has a particular nuance, untranslatable in other languages. In German, the third person singular of the verb "to be" and the third person singular of the verb "to eat" are very similar when written and almost identical when pronounced: *ist* (with one s) means "is"; with two (*isst*) it means "eats." So that the line is also a play on words: *Mann ist was er isst*"; when read, this means "Man is what he eats," but when spoken, it would seem to mean "Man is what he is" or "Man eats what he eats." What this suggests even more forcefully and paradoxically than in translation is the indivisible association of being and eating.

Seen this way, the line also works backward. By inverting the two verbs, the pronunciation remains the same but the meaning becomes "Man eats what he is." While proclaiming the supremacy of matter as the only true reality, Feuerbach thus declares simultaneously that this matter contains the ideas, thoughts, and culture of man. "Man eats what he is" means that food, on which man's identity depends, is not merely nutritional, but a reality rich in values, symbols, and meanings elaborated by the men and women who produced and prepared this food—in a word, a *cultural* reality.

Panettone is not just a composite of flour, sugar, raisins, and candied fruits; it is the very *idea* of Christmas. That idea was instilled in us by humans, to be consumed along with the flour and candied fruits that they themselves fabricated. The idea is indissoluble from the things that express it. Such an idea would not be possible in a society in which, for example, sugar, raisins, and candied fruits were commonplace, the basis of the daily diet.

Ludwig Feuerbach teaches us that there are no symbols without matter, nor even matter without symbols. For this reason, when we speak of *food and culture*, we are not speaking of two different realities, separate or even opposite, but of a single reality: Food *is* culture.

The invention of bread

Bread is not a "natural" food. It is the result of a complex process of production and technology, and of a refined alimentary civilization that learned to control and utilize nature's secrets. Bread is a truly great invention, whose secret is known only to man and to no other living creature. For this reason ancient Mediterranean societies viewed bread as a symbol not only of civilization but of the very identity of man, who distinguishes himself from other animals in that he knows how to construct his own food.

In the language of Homer and the ancient Greeks, "bread eaters" is synonymous with "men." Already in the *Poem of Gilgamesh,* a Sumerian text of the second millennium B.C., primitive man becomes civilized when he is no longer limited to consuming foods and drinks available in nature, such as wild herbs, water or milk, but begins to eat bread and drink wine, "artificial" products that he has come to know thanks to a woman who made a gift of them. The myth thus recognizes the female sex as primordial in the invention of agriculture, cooking, and, ultimately, cuisine.

In the heart of the Mediterranean, where the culture of bread originated (possibly in Egypt, possibly in Mesopotamia), Christian culture developed as well. It inherited that tradition, distinguishing bread as the ideal food not only for humans—as did Homer and the ancient Sumerians—but, more particularly, for Christian humans, "civilized" within the new faith. Through the miracle of the Eucharist, which refers to the Gospel account of the Last Supper, bread assumed an even greater significance as a sacred food, capable of putting man in contact with God. This is why during the Middle Ages, the period when Christianity took hold in Europe, the new religion prized and promoted the culture of bread. It became the primary food of Europeans, weighted with meanings not only nutritional, but symbolic.

Our daily bread

"Give us this day our daily bread" might appear to be the abandonment of divine providence, since what is implored is not manna, but bread. Manna falls from the sky; bread is made with work, so much work: cultivating the earth, planting seeds, waiting for them to mature, harvesting them, flailing them to separate the grain from the husk, preparing a suitable place (dry and cool) to store the grain, grinding it from time to time by manual skill or complex mills driven by wind or water, or more recently by electric motor, then stowing the flour in large and small sacks, they too kept in a cool, dry place; and finally mixing the flour with water, making the mixture rise by means of minuscule enzymes, dangerous by nature, which we have taught to behave properly and to work for us, waiting a while and then placing the dough in an oven, carefully calibrating the heat of the oven.

The bread is ready and will accompany other foods: the *companatico*, in Italian, meaning that which goes with bread, a term that presupposes the primary value of bread as the fundamental food. All languages deriving from Latin are familiar with it.

The amount of culture—that is, the knowledge and labor—contained in this highly complex procedure is incredible. It almost encapsulates the whole of human abilities, techniques and skills collected over millennia, allowing us to domesticate nature and transform the world. Bread has served to feed humanity, to fill the stomach, but it has also acquired fundamental symbolic values. Articulated in the forms, flavors, and modes of cooking, it gained an infinite number of variants, useful not only to break the monotony of daily life but, beyond that, to define spaces, times, collective identities: Each region, each community has its own bread; the calendar is marked by special breads that designate particular holidays. Bread has also served to establish and maintain relations with other men, and at times with the beyond.

As Jean-Louis Flandrin has indicated, the extraordinarily dense symbolism attributed to bread would be incomprehensible without the genuine excellence of the product. The amplitude and importance of the values bread has acquired in our culture would not be possible without its high intrinsic value—a taste, a flavor, a fragrance, an incomparable alimentary and gastronomic quality. Before becoming something else, bread was truly, concretely, the king of foods, and it could be that because men invested in it all their physical and mental energies.

To ask God to give us our daily bread means asking Him (whoever He may be) to let us be ourselves, to preserve that human identity, that dignity, that capacity to think and to make which we have laboriously managed to construct and transmit from one generation to another.

Even for the unreligious, this is indeed a very beautiful prayer: "Give us this day our daily bread."

Festive bread

The mechanism is simple. One takes an everyday food, enriches it with special ingredients, and modifies its taste. The magic is performed; the daily food becomes a festive food.

This is what happens when to flour and water one adds eggs, butter, and sugar, creating sweet bread, *pan dolce : panone, panettone, pane giallo, pan d'oro, pan di Natale....* The names are many, as are the recipes, but the meaning remains the same: On a feast day we need a different kind of bread.

The reduction of local variants, brought about by the food industry, is recent history. "The panettone of Milan, a Lombard specialty, has become the national Christmas cake," explained the *Guida gastronomica d'Italia* (the Gastronomic Guide of Italy), published by the Touring Club in 1931. Only a few years before, the father of Italian cuisine, Pellegrino Artusi, refused to include it in his cookbook out of devotion to the "panettone Marietta," made by his personal cook, and recommended for Christmas dinner "the bread of Bologna," derived from a traditional rustic recipe: "our peasants," remarked the agronomist Vincenzo Tanara, already in the seventeenth century made a "dough of flour with yeast, salt and water, to which are added raisins, honey-candied pumpkin, and pepper, and shaped into a large round loaf which they call Christmas bread."

The rustic, or even urban origin—always, however, associated with the working classes—seems to be a constant in defining the historic identity of this product. The improbable legends regarding the birth of the Milanese panettone seem to confirm this. Aside from the legend about the baker Toni, who is said to have given panettone its name ("pan di Toni"), another legend attributes its paternity to a Milanese noble by the name of Ughetto, who is uncharacteristically found at work outside his social setting. Having fallen in love with the daughter of a baker, Ughetto disguised himself as an apprentice in the baker's shop to be near his beloved and, after learning how to make the sweet bread, finally succeeded in winning over the baker through his taste buds.

Christmas breads, like all sweet breads, thus represent in the collective imagination a creation of the popular culture, almost a poor variation (because it is bread-based) on the taste of sweetness that triumphantly entered into upper-class cooking during the late Middle Ages and early Modern Era. Sweet dishes remained for a long time the privilege of the few, but a bit of sugar, or eventually honey, was not lacking to enhance simple cooking. This occurred parsimoniously, and not with all foods, nor every day: It was everyday bread that on occasion became transformed into a holiday bread.

Christmas bread is not only sweet but also stuffed with raisins and candied fruits, little surprises that are meant to signify plenty and well-being. Somewhat like Pinocchio's coins sown in the field of miracles, these little "seeds" are a hope of wealth, an augury of fertility.

Bread unites or divides?

An image deeply imprinted on our culture would doubtless reveal the heartwarming role that bread has played: hot fragrant bread coming out of the oven; bread broken and shared; bread surrounded by the family celebrating the ritual of survival, grateful to renew it day after day.

Bread has also been a cause of divisiveness and conflict in our history. The ancient Greeks regarded themselves as "civilized men" precisely because they were bread-eaters, different and distant from *others*, who chose to gather food in the forest and live on game and sheep-raising. For that very reason they were "barbarians." Juxtaposed over time on that ethnocentric ideology, which was incapable of understanding cultural diversity, are other images of a social nature, also based on the principle of separation. In the Roman period bread made of wheat was already distinguished from polenta made of spelt, the latter the traditional food of peasants, whereas the former was the food of the upper classes, who procured it in city bakeries. It was handed out by consuls, later by emperors, to urban plebs in order to ingratiate themselves and make city dwellers aware of their distinction from country people.

In the Middle Ages as well, bread was an important symbol of social difference. The diet of rural people was based primarily on thick or liquid soups and gruels of inferior grains (barley, oats, millet, yellow foxtail millet). Bread, when there was any, was dark, made of rye or spelt, cooked under embers rather than in an oven, in some cases to avoid the tax on the use of public ovens, which communities were obliged to use to bake bread. White bread made exclusively of wheat appeared only on the tables of patricians, urbanites, and monks. A twelfth-century text relates the story of a peasant who wanted to become a monk. When asked the reason for his vocation, as was customary, he unhesitatingly replied, "To eat white bread."

Similar distinctions have occurred in the modern era. In times of famine it was prohibited in the cities to sell *to peasants* white bread made of wheat.

Bread also served to divide religions. When Christianity chose bread as a sacramental food, placing it at the center of the liturgy of the Eucharist, this established a clean break with the Judaic tradition, which excluded fermented foods from the sacramental. When in 1054 the Greek church separated from the Roman church, one of the bones of contention was the accusation, made by the "orthodox" against the "catholic," that they had introduced into the Eucharistic rite a bread that was not really bread: an unleavened wafer that recalled instead the Hebraic tradition. Paradoxically, at about the same time, Western Christians, engaged in the anti-Islamic Crusades, regarded themselves as faithful custodians of the culture of bread, disdaining "Arab bread" (pita) as looking more like a half-baked focaccia than bread, according to a writer of the time.

Hail therefore to the integration of gastronomic cultures and customs that is taking place under our eyes. Hail to the varieties of bread that not only in the Mediterranean but all over Europe and even outside of it have gradually enriched our culinary heritage. Hail to the white bread that is on everyone's table, and to the dark bread on the tables of those who prefer it, without being forced into it. Hail also to those who, on occasion, want to exchange their usual loaf for a pita, and hail to the baker on the block who bakes it.

Divide meat, share soup

Filet of beef, chicken thighs, loin of pork, magret of duck, shoulder of lamb. . . . When dealing with a meat dish, the anatomy of the protagonist precedes any culinary description. To begin with, we select the cut we like, or what is our due: it is an ancient custom, attested since Homer, to offer the "best" part (according to parameters that vary in both time and space) to the master of the house or to the guest of honor. This ritual also transforms food into a sign of power and social prestige. The method of preparation is secondary. A piece of meat can be roasted, boiled, fried, braised. . . . What matters is that it be that, a piece of meat, whose shape is perfectly visible and recognizable as such.

In the case of salad or vegetables, this is of lesser concern, or none at all. Soup, gruel, polenta, purées have no shape; the shape they assume is that of the plate or the bowl. They cannot be *divided* into pieces but can merely be *shared* by the diners. Each one may have more, but not "the best part," which does not exist. The food in this case is equal for all, democratically equal. For this reason it tends to emphasize the solidarity of the group rather than the differences between individuals. In the Middle Ages, the porridge ladled out to monks had the secondary purpose of indicating the absence of hierarchy within the community. At the time of the French Revolution, the introduction of the *soupe populaire* (the hot soup offered by the Commune to its needy citizens) was a tangible means, within the concept of fraternity, of going beyond the old custom of helping the poor.

Soups of whatever kind are defined primarily not by their contents—the ingredients that compose them—but by the technique of their preparation. The recipe and kitchen work that operate on the components of the dish define their identity. The principal ingredient, when there is one, is secondary, almost an attribute: chickpea soup, broccoli soup, mashed potatoes, creamed spinach. More than a throwback to the basic product (as in the case of meats, unless they are meatballs), such expressions indicate a typology of food determined, for example, by its consistency: a soup can still be chewed and requires the recognition of its principal ingredients; mashed or creamed, in varying degrees of fineness, they can only be imagined in a homogeneous mass that in some way heralds the liquidity of the broth.

On the other hand, it is difficult or impossible to define the density of a *minestra,* a magical word coming out of a vast semantic spectrum that requires an infinity of different preparations. In this case, the word evokes not food but an *action*, an action of enormous convivial significance: *ministrare*, to minister, distribute; the act of offering and sharing food, ladling or pouring from one container (pan, pot, tureen) into the bowl or plate of each diner. In such an action, the need for nutrition is satisfied and at the same time sublimated in a powerful *idea*, that of representing the solidarity of people who gather around a table to celebrate the collective rite of survival in the warmth of a meal that brings them together.

Form and substance (discussion around a plate of pasta)

If thick soups, liquid soups or purées have no form of their own but only that of their container, pasta is form in its purest state, absolute form, the idea of form made concrete. Because without form there would be no pasta, at least not as we understand it.

"Pasta," is literally *"impasto,"* the magma of water and flour that has to be molded, waits to be shaped by the expert hands of the pasta maker that "feel" its warmth and that shape, lengthen, cut, fold, stuff, and seal it. That is "pasta," almost a clay with which one plays, getting one's hands sticky to create an object. "Pasta" is also the magma of durum wheat that requires machines to flatten, twist, or bore the dough to arrive at the ultimate stage of its particular identity. Italians call the final forms "pasta," preferring the singular to the plural to evoke the single origin of all of them. Other languages, like French, prefer to distinguish between them: the singular *pâte* indicates the common origin, the dough; the plural *pâtes* are the individual shapes ready for the pot.

The varieties of pasta have always been the pride of Italian gastronomy, ever since it entered our customs. The cookbooks of the fifteenth and sixteenth centuries were already aware of numerous shapes, and the names that we find in sixteenth-century texts are a tribute to the imagination and creativity of the pasta makers. "Pasta dishes," wrote Paolo Zacchia in 1636, "differ among themselves according to whether they are dried or fresh, larger or smaller, and whether they are made of wheat flour or something else. There are, moreover, various shapes: some are round, like *vermicelli* or *maccheroni*, among which some are hollow, some not; others are wide and flat, like *lasagne*; others are small and round, like those we call *millefanti*; others are flat but narrow like ribbons and are commonly known as *tagliolini*; others are short and thick, called *agnolini*; still others are longer and thicker, called *gnocchi*; and there are a thousand other shapes that make little difference with regard to their healthfulness."

A thousand shapes, practically the same in substance: "little difference."

And yet. . . .

And yet experience teaches us that different shapes of pasta, although alike in substance, produce different effects on the taste buds. Let's leave aside the sauces, which obviously make a difference. If we season pasta with nothing but butter and parmesan (the "classic" sauce for any pasta from the Middle Ages to the eighteenth century) and taste it, a forkful of spaghetti will not have the same flavor as a forkful of macaroni or of gnocchi. Chewing a strand of thin spaghetti will not be like chewing a thick one, and smooth macaroni will not have the same taste as ribbed macaroni. *Form* leads to different *flavor*. What is flavor if not the substance of food? (Medieval doctors were well aware of this; they considered flavor the means of "expressing" the nature of foods.) And so, *pace* to those who would have us believe that form is one thing and substance another; pasta seems made to show us the contrary, that the two interact in a more intimate fashion, almost to the point of coinciding. There is no form without substance, and no substance without form.

TWO

The Status of Foods

Esau's lentils, or how farmers defeated hunters

Esau is the hunter who roams the woods in search of game. His father, Isaac, "loves Esau because he likes game." His mother instead prefers the younger twin, Jacob, the farmer, a "peaceful and sedentary young man." Jacob is in the house having just cooked some steaming lentil soup. Esau returns from his meanderings, exhausted and famished. "Give me something to eat, some of that red stuff, because I'm so tired," he begs his brother. His brother strikes a deal: "Sell me your primogeniture and I will feed you." Hunger has the better of him and Jacob, in exchange for his brother's right of inheritance, "gives Esau bread and lentil soup."

The story in Genesis (XXV, 27–34) has a symbolic meaning that is all too clear. Agriculture has started to take over from more archaic economic forms, the peasant is overtaking the hunter, with cunning and even violence—the same violence that Cain, the farmer, inflicted on his brother Abel, the shepherd. These ancient Judaic stories, like those of other peoples and other civilizations, reveal the other face of agricultural society: "peaceful and sedentary" in appearance but in reality aggressive and invasive. Agriculture modifies the environment, alters the landscape. The farmer appropriates space in forests and displaces those who use them.

Even the alimentary message is clear. A good, steaming dish of home-cooked lentils is more secure and satisfying than a haunch of game.

Red lentils, the centerpiece of this biblical story, were especially appreciated in the ancient lands around the Mediterranean. Originating in eastern Syria and cultivated as early as nine thousand years ago, they became a staple in the diet of ancient Greeks and Romans. According to Atheneus, they were also used to make bread, and he can readily be trusted because from the Middle Ages to the Modern Era legumes were dried and ground, along with grains, to make flour for dough to be cooked in ovens, under embers or in a pan. A valuable food, and like all legumes nutritious, this longstanding usage has taught us to regard it as "the poor man's meat."

The lentils traditionally eaten in Italy on New Year's Day are a memory of this hallowed practice. Lentils are an augury of wealth and happiness. Perhaps it is only because their flat, round shape evokes the image of coins. Served with *zampone*, a pig's trotter stuffed with sausage meat, they could be merely an accompaniment; instead, they are the chief ingredient of the dish. To eat them on that day is an omen of a secure and comfortable tomorrow, as they were for Esau. Perhaps it is more than the magic of their form, their resemblance to money. It could also be the memory of that nasty story of Esau and Jacob that has imposed the idea of money onto that tiny legume—the birthright of inheritance bought with lentils.

Flour from spelt

There was a time, more than two thousand years ago, when Latins extracted most of their flour not from wheat, but from another grain called *farro*, spelt, from which the Italian word for flour, *farina*, comes. An archaic product, much older than wheat, of which it is a genetic mutation, spelt was a constant presence in the first civilizations of the Mediterranean basin, in Mesopotamia, in Egypt, and later in the Roman world. A coated grain—its kernels, like those of rice, are protected by a thin membrane that is eliminated through a process of polishing, unless intentionally kept whole, as in the case of brown rice or whole wheat. Ancient Romans thought that spelt was the ideal food for field workers. All kinds of gruel, soup, and porridge were made of it. Spelt, *puls* in Latin, was almost a national dish and became the culinary identity of Roman culture, just as Greeks were known by their flat bread made of barley.

Only around the second century B.C., as recorded by Pliny the Elder, did the first public ovens appear in Rome. That was when wheat, along with bread, replaced spelt and gruel in the Roman diet, but only in the cities; rural areas long remained faithful to their traditional eating habits. The cultivation of spelt was not abandoned, but continued to live side by side with its invasive neighbor, which was appreciated for its more delicate flavor, its finer flour, its higher gluten, allowing for better bread-making. During the Middle Ages spelt continued to be grown, above all in regions that remained attached to Roman models of production. In that respect, it is interesting to find spelt among the grains cultivated on the lands of Romagna during the high Middle Ages, which is precisely when the region took that name, signifying the continuing "Roman-ness" of those lands, later occupied by the Longobards. Like other "inferior" grains—millet, foxtail millet, sorghum, barley—spelt remained characteristic of a peasant diet, whereas wheat was a luxury product, reserved for the table of the upper classes and city dwellers. In this way a social contrast arose between upper-class bread made of wheat and the flour made of inferior grains, as well as black bread made of rye, in the diet of rural people.

Today the situation has changed radically. Having become universally available, wheat no longer denotes social differences. It is, rather, the "minor" grains—spelt and its companions—that denote diversity and prestige in new preparations (special breads, enriched pasta, multigrain biscuits) that, precisely because of these additions, are regarded as luxury products, sold at higher prices, and now esteemed as superior to the traditional products of white flour, even from the aspect of nutrition. The recovery of peasant foods has overturned symbols and meanings: the "poor" foods of the past have become the mark of new wealth.

"Inferior" grains?

I tasted a delicious bread made of organic grain that was stone ground, refined *ma non troppo*—a deep fragrance, delicate yet flavorful. The flour comes from a water mill in Hollange, Belgium, on the border with Luxembourg. The bread is sold at a small bakery in Brussels, run by the owner of the mill. The distinguishing feature of this bread is that it is made of spelt flour. The name of the bakery is *Le Pays de l'épautre* (The Land of Spelt).

Spelt is a genetic variant of *farro*, which is also known as "little spelt." The larger specie—called "large spelt" or simply "spelt"—was widely used throughout Europe during the Middle Ages as forage for horses and as human food, primarily by peasants.

During the Middle Ages the consumption of grains differed greatly among the social classes. Wheat, a demanding and delicate agriculture, was a prestigious and even luxurious product reserved for the aristocracy or for metropolitan merchants. More robust and prolific grains were cultivated for peasant consumption. White bread, a symbol of social advantage, was contrasted with the dark breads made from spelt and rye, the gruels of barley and millet, the porridges of oats and foxtail millet, all symbolic of the "peasant" diet. Medieval documents and literature always present these grains as signs of social baseness and thus labeled "inferior" or "minor."

In what way inferior? If the symbolism is beyond doubt, their inferiority with regard to taste is much less obvious and is perhaps the result of a cultural prejudice that nonetheless endured throughout the centuries, continuing all the way down to us. By that I mean that historians, when they describe a peasant food as coarse, rough or unrefined, are probably influenced by the negative image of those foods projected by the ruling classes ever since the Middle Ages.

To have tasted the spelt bread from the mill at Hollange was more than a pleasant gustatory experience. It was a way of rethinking the history of our peasants, which was a history of hunger and alimentary frustrations but also, at times, of pleasures and tasty dishes. We would be doing them a grave disservice if we held them incapable (as did the upper classes of the time) of enjoying food.

Liquid bread: from ale to beer

If you say *beer* you will at once think of northern countries, of the peoples who two thousand years ago surrounded the Roman Empire and, on the threshold of the Middle Ages, crossed over as conquerors, subduing Roman culture but acquiring a taste for wine. The meeting of the two traditions, the beer of the "north" and the wine of the "south," contributed to the enrichment of the European gastronomic experience, in the acceptance of this new drink that slowly invaded the territories of wine, initially limited to the central regions of the Continent, then spread all the way to the shores of the Mediterranean. More recently, in the twentieth century, this phenomenon was relaunched with increasing capacity of diffusion, thanks to the imposition of Anglo-Saxon lifestyles and models of consumption, carriers not only of new industrial ideas but also of the ancient Germanic culture.

Beer, however, comes not only from the north. The first to brew it were Mediterranean peoples, among the most ancient agricultural civilizations, in Egypt and Mesopotamia. Nor could it be otherwise, because beer is born of wheat and barley, which is to say products of the earth; it was born along with bread, another signal invention of Mediterranean peoples, and like bread is the product of fermenting grains, achieved in humid rather than dry surroundings. Beer is almost a kind of "liquid bread," and the Egyptian figurines of three and four thousand years ago, showing women busy making bread and mixing beer, juxtapose the two activities, both offsprings of the same economy and the same culture.

Liquid bread, but dense. The beer of the ancients was much denser than the one we know today. It was not really a solid drink, but something similar. Its flavor, produced by the carbohydrates, or sugars, of grains tended toward the sweet rather than the bitter, and to the sour, from spontaneous fermentation. These characteristics survived for a long time: Even Celts and Teutons, when they learned to produce this drink, "made in the manner of wine, but of barley and wheat" (as described by Tacitus in the second century), knew it as dense and sour-sweet.

Then something happened. During the Middle Ages, probably during the period of Charlemagne, someone (perhaps a monk assigned to making beer, or a peasant who gave him the idea) thought of adding hops to the fermenting liquid. Who knows how many experiments went into this. During the Middle Ages drinks— wine, beer—were treated more or less as a raw material with which to create new flavors, by mixing in herbs, flowers, spices, honey, flavorings. The blend was found pleasing and was perpetuated until it became definitive. The advantages of this innovation were at least two: Hops allowed the beer to become clarified and made it possible to decant it and strain the solid particles, so that it became at last a genuine drink, more thirst-quenching and better suited to accompanying a meal. Furthermore, hops introduced a slightly bitter taste that, blended with the sweet, was highly successful. This blending of contrasting flavors was typical of the taste of the time. As a further benefit, the addition of hops made it possible to keep beer longer.

This turning point caused the "new" beer to taste like a wholly different drink, and for that a new name was invented. Texts of the early Middle Ages called it *cervisia, cervogia,* a Gallo-Latin name that is still heard in the Spanish *cerveza.* From then on it was rebaptized under a new name of Germanic origin from which *bier, beer, bière, birra* were derived. As is usually the case, the history of names is the history of things.

The stench of garlic

A product of poverty, even more, a *mark* of poverty, which the upper classes scornfully disdained in our culinary tradition, was garlic. Let us begin with a text from the tenth century. An elderly pilgrim carrying a sack of garlic, onions, and leeks was returning to Rome and ran into a finicky monk by the name of Giovanni. "Let's get away from that stench," he said to his traveling companion, Odo, the abbot of Cluny. However, Odo taught him a lesson in humility: "For shame! He can eat these things and you can't even tolerate the smell?" The edifying moral of this episode does not conceal, but rather reveals the perception at the time of garlic, of its taste and its smell. In the imagination of the upper classes it was integral to the alimentary world of the peasant, rustic and coarse.

Such was the image of garlic in ancient times, and so it remained for centuries. A short story by Sabadino degli Arienti, a fourteenth-century Bolognese writer, places garlic at the very center of the plot, in a clash between two characters, the Duke of Ferrara and a peasant from the lower Po Valley by the name of Bondendo. This Bondendo had managed to get himself hired as the duke's valet, which led to a swelled head. He went so far as to claim that he had been nominated to become *cavaliere*, a knight. The duke decided to play a trick on him. He pretended to accede to the request for knighthood and one day invited his courtiers to the ceremony of investiture and the unveiling of the coat of arms designed expressly for the peasant and his family. The curtain was raised, revealing "a head of garlic on a field of azure," alongside a damsel who runs off holding her nose. The meaning was patently clear to one and all: A peasant you are and a peasant you will remain. Your peasant condition will always be recognizable, as it is now from the stench of garlic emanating from your body.

Garlic can nonetheless penetrate elite cuisine. All you need is a minor adjustment to "gentrify" it. The author himself, Sabadino, commenting on the story of Bondendo after confirming its meaning—how garlic reveals the rustic nature of those who eat it—could not help observing that even garlic can sometimes become "artificially well mannered" and enter into another gastronomic and symbolic world. This happens, Sabadino remarks, when "a roasted goose is stuffed with garlic," the garlic in this case is used to flavor a choice piece of meat, a luxury food. This is one of the "secrets" that the popular culinary patrimony uses to break down the ideological barriers of social privilege and that is eventually shared by the elite, according to instructions found in medieval and Renaissance cookbooks. Although intended for the upper classes of society—the nobility and upper bourgeoisie—ample allowance is made for popular culture. The mechanisms are simple: One takes a peasant recipe and ennobles it with the addition of expensive ingredients, inaccessible to most people (for example, sprinkling costly Eastern spices on a gruel of grains or legumes); serving a peasant food not as a main dish but merely as an accompaniment to some prestigious food; using peasant products as ingredients in a sumptuous dish (garlic-stuffed goose is an excellent example).

On an ideological level, taste is formed according to precise social boundaries. However, when an aristocrat appropriates a peasant dish or seasoning it readily transgresses those boundaries. The opposite can also occur: Sometimes the peasants accept values and flavors from the upper classes, they too modifying them according to their own customs. In this way, the tastes that reveal social distinctions merge into a common heritage.

The king's peas (and the peasant's too)

"The subject of peas continues: the impatience to eat them, the pleasure of having eaten them, the joy of being able to eat them again are the three points that concern our nobles for the past four days. There are ladies who, after having dined with the king, order peas to be prepared at home so as to be able to eat them before going to bed, at the risk of indigestion. It is a fashion, a furor." This letter from Madame de Maintenon, dated May 10, 1696, relates the passion for this green vegetable that raged in France at the court of Louis XIV at the end of the seventeenth century. "It is astounding," wrote a biographer of Colbert the previous year, "to see individuals so addicted to the pleasure of green peas [that they will] acquire them at enormous cost."

The peas that so greatly pleased the court of France were picked well before maturity: "The younger they are, the more exquisite they are," wrote Nicolas de Bonnefons, the king's chief steward. Peas were not the only vegetable in fashion at the time: Artichokes, zucchini, mushrooms, asparagus were equally appreciated in seventeenth-century haute cuisine, which progressively replaced the stronger flavors of the medieval tradition (those enormous platters of spice-covered meat) with milder, more delicate ones. Court gastronomy discovered new elements of distinction when the use of exotic products, such as spices, no longer served to mark differences; once trade was opened up by ocean liners, they became less costly and more accessible. Paradoxically, this created the rediscovery of products harking back to peasant fare.

To return to peas. A fashion, perhaps originating in Italy, where vegetables, beginning with the late Middle Ages, enjoyed a certain prestige even on patrician tables, which were not averse to presenting dishes from the peasant tradition, but with suitable adjustments. The recipe for "*piselli fricti in carne salata*" (fried peas in salted meat) included by Maestro Martino in the famous cookbook of the mid-fifteenth century is indeed reminiscent of peasant cuisine. First the peas are cooked in water, then thin slices of salted meat (half a finger long) are fried, and finally the peas are added to the meat and cooked together. This is the archetype of peas and prosciutto, which is still a dish typical of Italian gastronomy. A mark of distinction, indispensable in cookbooks destined for the upper classes, is provided by adding sugar and cinnamon, which complete Martino's recipe, along with *saba* (cooked must, or unfermented grape juice) and *agresto* (the juice of sour grapes). Another mark is the extremely early stage of the peas that are eaten "with the skin," or "just as they are," in other words in their entirety, along with the pod. Something like those of Louis XIV.

Already in the fourteenth century, Italian cookbooks anticipated recipes for peas with "salt pork." The southern *Liber de coquina* proposed cooking them in lard after being crushed with a spoon, to obtain a kind of thick and compact purée. The cooking water was then used for preparing a soup "in the French manner," seasoned with onion, crumbled bread and flavorful spices, and served with fragrant herbs in a hollowed-out round loaf.

Obviously, peasants could not allow themselves to forego the volume and the nutrition of full-grown peas by "wasting them" while they were still growing. They preferred to let them grow to maturity, even drying them and turning them into a flour to be mixed with other cereal flours or legumes. With this flour the peasants made *pappe* (gruels), polentas, and at times bread. It was primarily of the peasants (aside from his own monks) that Colombano, the sainted abbot of Bobbio, was thinking when he prodigiously succeeded in producing among the crags of the Apennines, "without anyone having sown them, between rocky fissures totally bereft of water," an extraordinary yearly flowering of peas, the *legumen Pis*, "which the peasants call *Herbilia*."

The potato, from emergency food to culinary specialty

When the Spanish conquistadores discovered the potato in Peru and introduced it in Europe, well into the sixteenth century, the unfamiliar tuber aroused general diffidence. Its "subterranean" nature did not grant it much prestige. Its taste was inconsistent, and even unsatisfying. It seemed to be a food less suited to humans than to animals. For a few centuries peasants refused to cultivate it, and when they changed their attitude it was out of need rather than choice. Given the extremely high yield of the potato compared with traditional crops, it could resolve a problem that was dramatically widespread at the time, namely hunger.

The coincidence is striking. In all regions of Europe, the cultivation of the potato always occurred in conjunction with years of famine. In 1778 the agronomist Giovanni Battarra recommended it as a means of vanquishing the hunger of the peasants, with a solicitude that reveals ancient prejudices. The potato, he writes, placing himself in the shoes of a peasant patriarch, "is an excellent food for humans no less than for animals," adding "how fortunate we are to be able to introduce extensive planting, for we will never again suffer from famine."

The potato was an emergency food in a situation of emergency. Between the eighteenth and nineteenth centuries, the progressive increase in population severely tested the social and economic system of Europe, which managed to survive at the cost of a general qualitative decline and harmful simplification of the peasant diet. It was also a problem of social disparity. Whereas quality foods continued to flow into urban markets and to appear on aristocratic and bourgeois tables, what remained for the peasantry was high-yield crops, such as corn or potatoes, which could fill the stomach and appease hunger—in the sense of dulling the sensation of hunger—with little concern for the quality or balance of the diet. In Mediterranean regions, the overwhelming preponderance of polenta, made of corn (which replaced many traditional dishes and preparations), resulted in a dreadful epidemic of pellagra, a disease typical of malnutrition. Different, but equally devastating, was the outcome of the dependence on the potato, in some cases total, which occurred in the countries of northern Europe. In Ireland, between 1845 and 1846, two failed potato harvests were enough to annihilate a peasant society that had improvidently based its system of survival on that product, and on that product *alone*. A third of the population was stricken with famine and infectious diseases, or forced to emigrate across the ocean.

Given these circumstances, it is understandable that the potato had to work hard to achieve gastronomic status in European kitchens. Only at the end of the nineteenth century was it finally able to efface its original stigma as poverty food, good at best for filling famine-stricken stomachs. Pellegrino Artusi, in the various editions of his *Scienza in cucina* (Science in the Kitchen), first published in 1891, included a number of recipes for artfully prepared potatoes destined for the well-to-do middle class of an Italy united merely thirty years earlier. Browned in butter or fried in oil, mashed into a purée or layered with truffles, the potato appears to have definitively found acceptance in the cuisine of the middle and upper classes of society. However, when Artusi proposed potato salad, he still felt the need to justify its presence: "Although made with potatoes," he wrote, "I assure you that this dish, in all its modesty, is worthy of praise." *Although made with potatoes.*

In the history of alimentary practices, necessity and pleasure travel separately at times, but more often their paths cross.

The eggplant, food of plebeians or Jews

Melanzana[1] is one of those words that are defined "connotatively" because they contain a judgment of the object represented. Its etymology leaves no room for equivocation, coming as it does from the Latin *mala insana*, unhealthful fruit, noxious to the health. The word appeared at the close of the Middle Ages to qualify negatively food that today delights us, and to catalog it among things to avoid. "*Pomo sdegnoso,*" contemptible apple, it was called by Bartolomeo Scappi, the most representative cook of Renaissance Italy.

---

[1] *Eggplant* in America, *aubergine* in England and France.

Why this "contempt"? Out of prejudice, it would seem, of a social nature. The eggplant rapidly became a culinary resource of poor people and was thus disdained by "good society."

Like other Asian plants, the eggplant was brought to Europe by the Arabs, who, during the Middle Ages, cultivated it in Sicily and Spain. Already mentioned in the stories of the thirteenth-century *Novellino*, there was an image of it in the *Tacuina sanitatis* of the fourteenth century. Diffidence toward it, which was long lasting, seemed consistently associated with its popular use. *"Pianta volgare"* the naturalist Pietro Andrea Mattioli called it in 1568, referring to its frequent use among the *volgo*, the populace: "It is eaten among the populace fried in oil with salt and pepper, like mushrooms." The following year we find similar testimony in the letter "on salad" by Costanzo Felici, addressed to his teacher and friend Ulisse Aldrovandi. He too indicates his distrust of the eggplant and does not share the enthusiasm of those who eat it "avidly, cooked for the most part in embers or on a grill, and even fried." These testimonies demonstrate, moreover, how widespread the use of eggplant was then (and probably centuries before) in daily cooking. During these decades similar distrust fell on the tomato, the new product of American origin that, Felici informs us, "those who crave and enjoy new things" were savoring "like the eggplant," fried in oil and seasoned with salt and pepper.

Most cookbooks of the Modern Era, which express the gastronomic culture of the upper classes, very rarely include eggplant. Its controversial image, related to a status of absolute social and cultural marginality, is confirmed and, even more, amplified, accentuated in a way, by the particular attention that it seems to enjoy in Jewish cooking. In 1631 the treatise on carving by Antonio Frugoli conjoins Jews with plebeians, maintaining that the eggplant "should not be eaten other than by people of the lower class or by Jews." The same attribution is repeated a decade later by the agronomist Vincenzo Tanara, who defines the eggplant as "food for rural areas . . . commonly consumed by domestics and by Jews."

This singular label can still be found at the end of the nineteenth century, in *Science in the Kitchen* by Artusi, who by then had reversed the meaning, remarking that *i petonciani* (as he called eggplants) "were held in contempt as a food of Jews," which only proves that "in this as in other things of greater importance, [they] always had a better nose than Christians."

The bread tree

"*Chestnuts* are the bread of the poor," declares a Tuscan statute of the fifteenth century. Two centuries later, the Emilian Giacomo Castelvetro pointed out that "thousands of our mountain people nourish themselves with this fruit as a substitute for bread, which they never, or hardly ever, see."

The fate of these two products, chestnuts and bread, evolved in parallel ways. There is a moment in the history of Italy and Europe—the mid-centuries of the Middle Ages, between the tenth and the twelfth—when the increased population no longer chose to live on a forest-based economy. What ensued was a veritable mutation of the environment. In plains regions, progressive deforestation made way for fields of grain. In mountainous regions, where grain is hard to cultivate, forests did not disappear but were transformed. Oak trees, predominant in earlier centuries and whose acorns fostered a large production of pork, were largely replaced by "cultivated" trees that provide a fruit different from a kernel of grain yet fundamentally similar: the chestnut. Once dried, it can be milled into flour. Although the taste is not the same, its alimentary uses are: bread, polenta, cakes. . . . For this reason, in Mediterranean countries the chestnut is called the "bread tree." Its fruit is the bread of that tree.

Today chestnuts are a typical seasonal fruit. In the past, their consumption was not limited to the time of their harvest. Effective techniques of preservation allowed them to be stored for long periods, either in their shell or heat-dried. "In our mountain regions," wrote the sixteenth-century Brescian agronomist Agostino Gallo, "a large segment of the population lives exclusively on this fruit." In 1553, the Captain of the Pistoian Mountains remarked that the inhabitants of Cutigliano are "extremely poor and seven-eighths of them eat only *castagnacci*[2] *all year long.*" In less impoverished zones and in years of lesser hardship, the particular preservability of this product led to a flourishing trade. Chestnuts wound up in distant markets (even beyond the Alps and beyond the Mediterranean) and remained on the market for many months, until the following spring. Vincenzo Tanara, a Bolognese agronomist of the seventeenth century, observed that chestnuts could be served as late as summer, "out of exoticism." From hunger to satiety, the distance is shorter than it would seem.

In earlier centuries, the gastronomy of the chestnut appears to have been richer and more imaginative than today. Castore Durante, in the sixteenth century, recalls the custom of cooking them "in a pot with oil, pepper, salt, and orange juice." Orange juice recurs in Giacomo Castelvetro, who recommends that roasted chestnuts be salted and peppered, and reports that poultry was stuffed with chestnuts (after having been boiled in milk): "and they are very good, and are used to stuff capons, geese and turkeys that are to be roasted, along with dried plums, raisins and bread crumbs." This is a European recipe that would have found particular favor on the American continent.

Vincenzo Tanara collected many local recipes (such as this one from Piedmont, in which chestnuts are cooked in wine "with fennel, cinnamon, nutmeg, and other spices") devoting much attention to cakes, *castagnacci,* and fritters of various ingredients. For his taste, he claims to prefer simple confections: "*castagnacci,* cooked between round stone tiles the thickness of a finger and piping hot, or better yet, red-hot, made of next to nothing and still

---

[2] A baked product made of chestnut flour, which can be a bread, a cake, or a fritter.

warm when eaten, are an exquisite food, accompanied by a side dish of a hearty appetite."

The peaches of Messer Lippo

When I bite into a peach I cannot help but think of Zuco Padella.

Zuco Padella was a peasant about whom Sabadino degli Arienti, a Bolognese notary and literary figure, wrote in 1495 in a collection of stories dedicated to the Duke of Ferrara, Ercole d'Este. Sabadino imagines, in the manner of the *Decameron*, that a brigade of gentlemen and ladies from Bologna set off during the summer for the baths of Porretti, entertaining themselves in such pleasant pastimes as storytelling. In these *Porrettane*, simple folk also appear, always seen through the eyes of the noble companions; their role is to be humble, humiliated, mocked. The distance between the classes is a fundamental postulate of the culture of the ruling classes (of that period, of course, Manzoni would say) and this is expressed in the codes of eating behavior, the way of thinking about foods and their "appropriate" social destination.

Peaches, like other delicate fruits, are not peasant food, being reserved for the elite, but occasionally peasants did not play according to the rules. Sabadino explains this to us in a fable whose characters are a peasant, Zuco Padella, and a patrician, messer Lippo Ghisilieri.

Lippo had a splendid garden filled with fruit, "especially gorgeous peaches," jealously protected by shrubbery and ditches. Nonetheless, "almost every night" Zuco Padella made his way through the bushes, reached the peach trees, and carried away some fruit. This was not an occasional theft motivated by need or hunger, but rather a systematic and persistent challenge to the privilege of class.

Messer Lippo, to expose the impudent transgressor, had a series of traps dug in the earth and lined with nails pointed upward. At night, when Zuco entered the garden, "his big toe stepped on one of those nails." Even though he was injured, he did not give up. The following night, he put on stilts attached to "horseshoes" to avoid puncturing his toes, "and so that it would look as though a donkey were eating the peaches." He then carried off another load of fruit and went home unhurt.

This raised the stakes, forcing the orchard owner to invent new strategies. He had all the peaches picked except for fhose on one tree, around which he had a large hole dug "like a pitfall for catching wolves." For three nights he personally kept guard and at last Zuco Padella arrived on his stilts. He went directly to the tree heavy with peaches and fell into the ditch, "nearly breaking his neck." Lippo ordered his servants to bring a basin of boiling water and empty it into the pit. The peasant began to scream: "Have pity, have pity!" and was thus revealed. "I thought I had caught a wolf with four legs, not two," Lippo sarcastically remarked and, adding insult to injury, said, "I wanted to catch a wolf but instead I caught the donkey who was eating my peaches." The moral was accompanied by words of arrogant contempt: "Villainous thief that you are! May a thousand leeches fall upon you!"

The ferocity of this combat—a full-scale war—equals the harshness of an ideological system that claimed to demonstrate through the diversity of foods the differences between men and the preservation of the social order: each one in his place, patricians to command and peasants to obey. "Next time," messer Lippo concludes sententiously, "leave my fruit alone and eat your own: turnips, garlic, leeks, onions, and shallots, along with sorghum bread. Peaches are only for *my equals*."[3]

I think of Zuco Padella—who ingeniously and clumsily sought to attack the privilege of class—as a hero of social redemption, and the next time I have sliced peaches I will gratefully raise my bowl to him.

---

[3] A pun may have been intended: in the plural, *scalogne* are shallots, but *scalogna* in the singular means "bad luck."

Five hundred pears

Jean-Baptiste de la Quintinie, gardener to the Sun King, Louis XIV, prided himself on having cultivated 500 species of pears, their various growing seasons spaced out over the year so that, in theory, His Majesty could have a different kind of pear every day. This prodigious horticulturist gave an account of his virtuosity in a treatise on pomology (*Instruction pour les jardins fruitiers et potagers*) published in 1690.

The Sun King's passion for pears was shared by much of European nobility. The "pear mania," as a historian labeled it, signaled the predilections and tastes of the upper classes. Court cookbooks contain many ways to use pears. Specialized manuals on topiary demonstrate how to prune pear trees and shape them into attractive and unusual shapes.

In some ways this was the final chapter of a story that had begun centuries earlier, a story of tastes and flavors, but also of symbols and images. From the end of the Middle Ages, fruit had become an established sign of lordly gourmandise—in particular, delicate, perishable fruit, like the pear. Fruit evoked alimentary luxury, not choices linked to the daily struggle against hunger, but the pleasures of the unnecessary.

Medieval doctors generally discouraged the consumption of fresh fruit. They warned against the excessive "coldness" of its nature, but if someone was determined to indulge in the pleasure of gluttony and social prestige, a few accommodations were required. On the principle of "temperament," which entered the science of the time from the Hippocratic and Galenical tradition (the natural imbalance of foods must be righted with appropriate compensations), coldness had to be "heated," and two methods were recommended: either serve fruit with a full-bodied wine or cook it over the fire, better yet, cook it in wine. From these teachings and practices arose proverbial locutions that remained alive in various European languages: "After a pear, wine," is a saying documented in France and in England as of the fifteenth century.

Other texts insist on the need for cooking: "*Se velen la pera è detta, sia la pera maladetta*," declares a text from the medical school of Salerno; "*ma quando è cotta, ad antidoto è ridotta*" (it is said if the pear is poisonous, let the pear be damned, but when cooked it is reduced to an antidote). A pear cooked in wine, which still appears at the end of many menus today, particularly in popular circles, is the descendant of this ancient culture and is fortunately still in our own, because it has remained valid on the level of taste.

Little by little dietary convictions became modified because foods themselves became modified. The seventeenth-century "mania" for pears was not just the reappearance of a gastronomic and symbolic model from the Middle Ages. It was also the result of changes made to the primary matter through the patient work of horticulturists, farmers, agronomists. Many of them remain anonymous and unknown, and others (like the gardener of Louis XIV) were honored by the court and proud enough of their profession to want to leave a memory of it in ponderous works of theoretical reflections and practical teachings. The species multiplied and fruit became increasingly pleasing and sweet, its flavor immediately indicating a new identity.

The culture of a period can also be measured by the importance and inventiveness of its attitude toward food. Of the five hundred species of pears described by Quintinie in his *Instruction*, how many are we able to identify today?

To die for a melon

Pope Paul II died of a sudden apoplectic attack the night of July 26, 1471. His doctors attributed this to a melon binge the evening before. After having spent the day in consistory, the pontiff dined late (around ten) on "three melons, not too large" and other things "of meager substance, as had become his habit over the past few months." The account of this event, written in these words by Nicodemo di Pontremoli in a letter to the Duke of

Milan, reveals an attitude of great suspicion toward this fruit, capable of causing not only indigestion but even death. The alimentary imprudence of the pontiff was recalled as well in a biography by the humanist Bartolomeo Sacchi, known as Platina: "He was extremely fond of melons," Sacchi wrote, "and it is believed this is what provoked the apoplexy that took his life. As it happened, the evening before he died he had eaten two melons, and big ones moreover." Apart from the discrepancy of number and size, the link between the two events is treated, here too, as credible and expectable.

How did this diffidence toward melons arise?

The coolness and juiciness of the fruit, which makes them desirable during the heat of summer, were qualities that medieval medicine regarded as negative on the dietary scale. It was thought that this "coldness," common to many fruits, undermined the natural heat of the organism and dangerously upset the equilibrium of the bodily humors, shifting them toward cold. This judgment, based on principles of Galenical medicine, might also be related to the fruits themselves, which were then less sweet than they are today, in some cases still very close to their wild state. Doctors commonly advised people to eat little of them and, if possible, to avoid them entirely. Melons in particular were held to be the most toxic of all fruits.

However, if one wanted to eat a melon, there was no dearth of strategies to protect the health. The coldness of a fruit could be tempered by the heat of the fire and by wine.

It is not hard to see in this scientific tradition the meaning, the ideology so to speak, of a custom so typically French as accompanying melon with a glass of strong sweet wine (port, for example). Nor is it hard to see the meaning of a custom so typically Italian (now popular throughout the world) as serving melon with prosciutto, an absolute *must* on the summer menu. It hardly matters that today, thanks to the scientific work on botanical species of the past centuries, melons have become extremely sweet and, from the optic of a medieval doctor, perhaps less dangerous.

Since these customs took root long ago and are enjoyable, there is no reason to give them up. Melons should nonetheless be eaten with measure. Three whole melons are indeed too many, even if eaten with prosciutto or port. "Meager substance" is also a question of quantity.

Strawberries in November

In 1655 Queen Christina of Sweden traveled down to Italy on her way to Rome, after having converted to Catholicism and abdicated her throne. On November 27th she stopped in Mantua, where she was honored at the Gonzaga court with a sumptuous banquet prepared by Bartolomeo Stefani, one of the most famous chefs of the period. About that banquet we know everything there is to know because Stefani described it himself seven years later in an appendix to one of his cook books, *L'arte di ben cucinare* (*The Art of Good Cooking*). He recounted it with pride as one of the greatest moments of his brilliant career.

In the long list of dishes presented on that occasion, there is one that immediately draws our attention. As an appetizer, there were "*fraghe,*[4] rinsed with white wine and served with sugar on top." A very simple dish, although embellished with little sugar sculptures, as was common on the Baroque table—sculptures with a theme: "around the edge of the plate, shells made of sugar filled with these strawberries, alternating with birds made of marzipan, which seemed about to peck at the fruit."

It is not surprising to see strawberries with sugar and marzipan served at the beginning of a meal. Seventeenth-century cuisine, in the wake of Renaissance tastes, had an appetite for sweets at every meal and put sugar in everything. As for the strawberries, it is hard to say whether they were cultivated or wild. In Stefani's day, experiments had already begun on crossing wild strawberries

---

[4] *Fragole*, in modern Italian, strawberries.

(the only ones known during the Middle Ages) with the new species brought from America. From these mutations were born the various types of large strawberries, like those selected for Louis XIV by his gardener, Jean de la Quintinie, from the gardens of Versailles at the close of the century. Here we are barely at the beginning of a story (that of large strawberries) that will evolve only in a later period, from the eighteenth and nineteenth centuries on. Seventeenth-century taste was still accustomed to wild strawberries, and it is more than likely that those were the ones served at the banquet in Mantua in 1655.

Let us rather look at the date: November 27th. Strawberries were absolutely out of season. With an achievement like that opening dish, the Gonzaga chef had already impressed his illustrious guest. Selected meats and succulent preparations would have followed, but the success of the banquet was assured from the outset. At that time, as in the Middle Ages and the Renaissance, to offer foods that were out of season conferred prestige on the host (as Stefani himself liked to point out when commenting on his culinary choices), although everyone knew *"Il frutto non è buon, fuori di stagion,"* (fruit is not good out of season), as proclaimed in a sixteenth-century proverb.

If the fruit is not good, so what? One does not eat for pleasure alone. A princely table is supposed above all to show wealth, power, the ability to bring together priceless resources and ingredients. In a world in which it was normal to respect the seasonality of produce, even an obligation, not to do so was a mark of distinction.

In this ancient wish to disrupt the seasonal rhythms, seen as a "peasant" restriction, we can recognize the root of certain modern practices, no longer elitist but popular. Except that today, the reasons for the prestige have become invalid: to eat strawberries out of season is no longer a privilege reserved for a few. We might define this as a democratic achievement, which is nonetheless accompanied by the collective loss of seasonality, undermined by the rhythms of industry and the globalization of food production. That very culture, paradoxically, gave Stefani a feeling of infraction.

To retrieve it as a strong and positive value, overturning the paradigms of alimentary luxury, would be a small cultural revolution even to the advantage of our pleasure. Because *"Il frutto non è buon, fuori di stagion."*

Watermelons and cucumbers

"Watermelons[5] are common during the summer" and are eaten primarily "to quench the thirst," since they provide no nutritive value or "pleasure." Thus writes the botanist Costanzo Felici around 1570, with little interest in a product that he clearly evaluates as "minor" in terms of nutrition. Even thirst warrants consideration, and for that, watermelons are excellent, given their "very watery" composition, some of them very sweet, "which for that reason are called *cucumeri zuccarini,*" sugary watermelons.

The history of food does not tell us much about watermelons and related plants, partly because of the difficulty of clarifying an uncertain, ambiguous terminology. When reference is made to this plant, the texts that discuss it (for the most part treatises on dietetics or botany) struggle to find authoritative material, because it is not even possible to identify the watermelon in the classical literature. In 1627, for example, Salvatore Massonio (author of an interesting work on salads and vegetables) quotes Dioscorides to distinguish between domestic and wild watermelons. The latter, "not at all nutritious," are of use only medicinally "and are horribly bitter to the taste." The others instead "are useful to the stomach and the body." To which plant is Dioscorides referring, watermelons or cucumbers, or still others? Massonio confesses that he does not understand and so prefers to gloss over the *auctoritates* and go directly to the practice and language of his contemporaries: "For clarity . . . let us accept as watermelons what Lombards call

---

[5] *Cucumeri* in the original text, *cocomeri* in modern Italian; also popularly called *angurie.*

cocomeri, known as *cedriuoli* in Tuscany and in Rome, and in our region of Aquila[6] by the name of *melangole.*" The Spanish, however, call it *peponi* and use it, Amato Lusitano claims, to cool the body both internally and externally: "We make a practice of using the outer cut part to cool the forehead during the hottest hours of the day, when we also eat it to achieve the same effect." Even Bartolomeo Sacchi, the fifteenth-century humanist known as Platina, uses the term *popone* to indicate watermelons, "different from melons, the latter being almost round and ribbed, whereas the others are oblong."

Like most things, the watermelon has some virtues: It purges the kidneys and the bladder, "reduces inflammation of the stomach and gives a certain relief to the intestines," so long as the seeds are removed. Generally, however, it slows the digestion, which is to say the process of "cooking" the food in the stomach, which requires heat and dryness, characteristics diametrically opposed to those of the watermelon. "*Il popone,*" Platina writes, "is doubtless tasty, but is hard to digest because it is cold and wet." For that reason one is advised to eat it on an empty stomach, "otherwise it slows the digestion." It is also better to accompany it with wine rather than water, because water would only add more cold and more moisture, whereas wine functions in the opposite way. One can also view this instinctively: "I follow nature," Platina writes, "which, after one has eaten watermelon, is inclined to want wine, and good wine, because it is almost an antidote to the rawness and coldness of the watermelon."

Sweet as a fig

The fig means sweetness. Quintessence of the Mediterranean landscape and spirit, this plant and fruit are accompanied by the

---

[6] Of which Massonio was a native.

sweetest of images, in both its figurative and literal sense, passed down by ancient literature, from Mesopotamian to biblical texts and on down to Greek and Latin classics. "Sweet as a fig," the connection fig–sweet is as automatic as it is validated by an illustrious tradition.

For a long time the fascination with sweetness was more intense and more complex than it is today for us. It was not a flavor easily produced before the era of sugar, which started at the end of the Middle Ages and exploded in modern times. Only honey had been able to provide sweetness, which was why particular attention was given to fruits that, fresh or dry—dates, raisins, figs—could serve as a substitute. The many varieties of figs, each with its own characteristics, were listed in ancient texts by such agronomists as Cato and Columella, and later in the great encyclopedia by Pliny. Some figs took their name from their native territory: Chios, Syria, Africa, Numidia, Caria. . . . Others from historical figures who in some way had associated the fig with their name: livian (Livy), pompeian (Pompey), calpurnian (Calpurnia). Still others from the time or modality of their growth: late or early figs; spring, summer, or autumnal figs; figs that had a single or a double growing season. Medieval texts provide further proof of these distinctions: the sixteenth-century botanist Constanzo Felici could only say "there are so many varieties it makes one dizzy merely to think about it."

So many species, but one common trait: sweetness. This is an extraordinary virtue because, on the scale of flavors, sweet was considered the most perfect, the most balanced, the most "suited" to human health. According to the dietary thinking that continued from Hippocrates to Galen, sweet somehow amalgamated the other flavors, "tempered" them, modified their characteristics by forcing them to the point where their qualities met and canceled each other, thereby enhancing itself in the process. Someone has written that the basic principle of ancient and medieval cuisine lay in a process of sweetening, of reducing each individual flavor to a level of equilibrium.

The fig, which in its nature contained this desired sweetness, seemed ideally made to represent perfection. Ancient and medieval doctors, always suspicious about fruit (held to be too acid, and in the Galenic classification, too "cold" for the digestive needs of the stomach), were obliged to make an exception when it came to figs. Even they, like all other fruits, could provoke bad humors, but it had to be admitted that "fresh figs, especially those ripe ones that tend toward the warm and moist, are not harmful to the health." So wrote Platina, in his famous book *On Safe Pleasure and Good Health.*

Certain traditional proverbs, reaching down to the roots of medieval food culture, confirm this diversity of the fig. Whereas so many fruits, because of their coldness, had to be "corrected" in the opinion of dietetic science (which later passed into the proverbial), the fig did not require any correction. It could therefore be accompanied by water, a neutral and tasteless substance, minimally invasive on the nutritional level, capable if anything of dissolving the strength and heat of the fig, To quote from the repertory of Italian proverbs: "To the fig, water; to the pear, wine"; "To the peach, wine; to the fig, water." It is recommended that the fig be peeled before eating: "For a friend, peel the fig."

 THREE

Adventures in Cooking

From raw to cooked (and back)

Raw is synonymous with "nature." Claude Lévi-Strauss taught us this when he was analyzing the alimentary attitudes and habits of peoples without a written language. We learned the same lesson from ancient texts that inevitably associated uncooked food with barbarity. The myth of Prometheus, who stole the secret of fire from the gods and gave it to humans, established the idea of culture as the ability to transform nature, of which cooking is an essential dimension. This is why Greeks and Romans, wishing to be seen as the trustees of civilization, chose to describe *the others*, the "barbarians," as eaters of raw meat: Tacitus's Germans (who "eat only wild fruit and freshly killed game"), and Ammiano Marcellino's Huns (who merely warm a cut of meat between the back of their horse and their own bottom) are the prototypes of a mental model that lasted for centuries, so that still in the Middle Ages people who did not cook their meat (the Scandinavians of Paul the Deacon) or their grains (Procopius's Moors) were described as "barbarians." Christian hermits, in their radical refutation of "the world" and "civilization," elected to eat only raw, and wild, plants. The knight Yvain, a courtier of King Arthur, driven mad by his wife's rejection when he was away at war too long, wanders into the forest, where he throws off all trace of courtly manners and begins living exclusively on raw meat. Later, he slowly returns to his knightly state, and the first sign of his recovery is his return to cooked food prepared for him, curiously enough, by a hermit, as recounted by Chrétien de Troyes in his famous twelfth-century romance *Yvain, the Knight with the Lion.*

Contrasted with this is the diffidence of medical science toward raw food. Such views are confirmed by cookbooks, entirely oriented toward the practices of cooking food: Whatever comes to the table must be cooked, not only meat and fish, but also fruit, vegetables, even cheese, dried and salted meats, truffles. There are a few exceptions: The sixth-century doctor Anthimus alludes to the practice of the Franks of eating raw lard to cure stomach afflictions, and he remarks, amazed though not scandalized, that people who habitually eat raw meat generally enjoy good health. The broadest acceptance of raw food can be seen in the exclusively Italian taste for raw vegetables, to which, during the sixteenth and seventeenth centuries, treatises were devoted by Costanzo Felici, Salvatore Massonio, and Giacomo Castelvetro (particularly noteworthy is the title of Castelvetro's work dedicated to "all roots, all herbs and all fruits, whether *raw or cooked,* eaten in Italy").

Two major changes accompanied the definitive rehabilitation of raw food in later gastronomy. One was of a philosophical nature: Enlightenment and Romantic thinking saw nature for the first time, though from different angles, as something beneficent, as an "original good" (Rousseau comes to mind) that should not be modified but kept as is. The other was scientific: Only in the nineteenth century was it discovered that there are certain components in food essential for nutritional balance, vitamins, and that they are lost in cooking. Added to that is the development of techniques for conservation, more effective and secure than ever before. In this way our perspective has been overturned. We no longer regard raw food as an archaic vestige but as a mark of alimentary modernity. The itinerary of raw to cooked seems to be on the road back.

The perfect recipe

At the University of Leeds in England a group of researchers set out to determine scientifically the rules for making "the perfect sandwich": size of the slices of bread, thickness of the bacon (I might have preferred prosciutto), the exact number of minutes the bacon should be grilled. After hundreds of experiments and tastings, the ideal recipe, or rather, the formula, was achieved.

I confess my perplexity in the face of initiatives like these and of the philosophy that motivates the discovery of the perfect canon, the right recipe, the rule to follow. I have always been diffident about any pretension of codification, standardization, uniformity: the "true" recipe for meat sauce, the "true" dimensions for tagliatelle, the "true" filling for tortellini. . . . There is too much ambiguity in that terrible adjective *true* that would brand as *false* any variation, any inventiveness, any departure from the rule. Speaking of tagliatelle and tortellini brings up the question of tradition, which would seem to be the exact opposite of the scientific approach of the Leeds experiment mentioned earlier. In reality, the two perspectives are very much alike.

Cuisine consists above all in freedom, differences, variations. Cooks of the past knew that only too well when they committed their recipes to paper, never dreaming that those were the "true" ones, to be followed line by line. On the contrary, they left open to the procedure and inventiveness of each individual the freedom "to vary flavors and colors" (as we read in an Italian text of the fourteenth century), or to respect the tastes of the diners, or the customs of the locality. Even the greatest professionals (such as Bartolomeo Scappi, author of the most important cookbook of the Italian Renaissance) limited themselves to "relating" their recipes, offering more than one for each type of food, precisely to indicate the nonexistence of an obligatory code to be followed. Let us not even mention home cooking, anarchic by definition, consisting in recipes that vary from family to family.

What I mean to say is that in cooking one must be careful when talking about rules. Rules there must indeed be: Fundamentals of cooking techniques, typology of seasonings, principles of what goes together, and above all a knowledge of products—these are indispensable premises for serious work. This applies to fundamentals, which is why my favorite kitchen manual is a precious little book written by Gualtiero Marchesi[1] a few years ago in which no recipe is to be found, merely the explanation of basic techniques for keeping meat tender, preventing risotto from getting mushy, retaining the flavor of vegetables. . . . Beyond that, freedom reigns.

To look for "the true recipe" (be it grandmother's tagliatelle or the Leeds sandwich) presupposes an authoritarian attitude that is ill suited to the pleasure of food.

Cappelletti and tortellini: the retro-taste of history

How do culinary tastes and traditions arise? In answer to a question like this, certain episodes seem ideally suited to demonstrate the importance of history as an integral element in local identities.

Let us consider the taste for lamb, which exists only in certain parts of Italy. This is related in part to environmental differences: the presence of grazing land in the center–south and on the Mediterranean islands of Sardinia and Sicily has historically favored the spread of sheep-raising, whereas in the north and in the Po Valley, the presence of forests made raising pigs the better choice. Other reasons, of a cultural nature, can also explain the geography of tastes. The tradition of the pig played a central role in the alimentary culture of the Germanic populations that occupied a large part of Italy during the Middle Ages, encouraging a predilection

---

[1] Chef of the eponymous three-star restaurant in Milan.

for pork even in the south. The sheep was the animal best suited to Roman husbandry and can even be found in the north, in areas that remained tied for a longer period to Roman traditions of production and culture.

Let us consider the case of Emilia-Romagna, a region that owes its double name to the double history that determined it during the Middle Ages. Emilia was early occupied by the Longobards, who invaded Italy in the seventh century. Romania, "land of the Romans,"[2] took its name at that particular time because for centuries it had resisted the Longobard conquest, and thus remained under the imperial control of Byzantium, the "new Rome," administered by the governor in Ravenna. These various political and administrative factors had significant effects on alimentary traditions as well. A taste for lamb or mutton never took hold north of Bologna, whereas it is very characteristic of the gastronomic tradition of Romagna (a tradition consolidated after World War II by the arrival of many Sardinian shepherds in the Apennines). Halfway between these two models lies Bologna, where castrated sheep are eaten as an "exotic" specialty: *"Castrato di Romagna"* can be seen on signs in the market. Beyond possibilities related to landscape, environment, or climate, such customs can only be seen in the contrasts between Longobards and Byzantines established during the Middle Ages.

The difference between the two cultures also appears in the way that cappelletti and tortellini are filled according to the typical traditions of the two regions. In Emilia, tortellini are filled with meat (reflecting an indigenous pork culture). In Romagna, cappelletti are filled with cheese (reflecting a sheep culture—the ewe being the provider of milk and cheese—which precedes a meat culture). Although apparently similar, the two dishes mirror separate histories in which common elements and differences can be seen. What they have in common is the great Italian tradition of filled pasta

---

[2] Later spelled Romagna.

dough, the outgrowth of a shared culture born between the Middle Ages and the Renaissance. What separates them are the local "declensions" of stuffings, which hark back to different histories and traditions.

This microhistory, revelatory as are so many others, shows us the extraordinary cultural density that lies behind culinary traditions. Behind every dish, every flavor, there is another "historical retro-taste" that is worth knowing and tasting.

Macaroni, or is it gnocchi?

The macaroni[3] immortalized in a famous novella by Boccaccio were in fact gnocchi. They flowed (so the ingenuous Calandrino was led to believe) down the sides of the "mountain made entirely of grated parmesan cheese" in the middle of the Land of Bengodì[4] after having been cooked in a huge cauldron up on the summit. Down below, "the more one ate, the more there was." It was Luigi Messedagia, the first real historian of Italian cuisine, who explained that those macaroni were really gnocchi, because originally that was the meaning of the word—from maccare, or ammaccare, to knead. A dish dear to the peasantry, gnocchi were like a variation of polenta, pultes, pulmenta. The cookbooks of the Late Middle Ages and Renaissance provide us with the first, utterly simple, recipes: flour or bread crumbs, mixed with cheese or egg yolks, to obtain dumplings cooked in boiling water (or better yet, in capon broth, as practiced in Bengodì).

If this was the popular dream, not even the cooks of Renaissance courts thought of giving it up. Cristoforo Messisbugo prepared gnocchi for the Este table in Ferrara, and Bartolomeo Scappi (who worked in Rome in the kitchens of the pope) remembered these "macaroni, called gnocchi," which were "made of flour, the

---

[3] Spelled maccheroni in Italian,
[4] From ben, good, and, godere, to enjoy, i.e., the land of pleasure.

crumb of bread and boiling water, grated cheese on top, boiled, covered with garlic sauce."

Later, potatoes arrived from America, but even that new product was incorporated into the tradition and entered into the composition of gnocchi, which, as of the eighteenth century, acquired the mild flavor that is most familiar today—another example among many showing how culinary culture succeeds in reworking innovations and adapting them to its own history.

This is not why medieval gnocchi disappeared. Grated bread and flour, mixed and enriched with a variety of ingredients and flavors, continue to be the ingredients in recipes for *canderli* or *knödel* (the same etymology as *gnocchi*) that are still made in Alpine areas in different forms, be it in broth or dry, sauced in butter, grated cheese, and sweet spices (cinnamon, nutmeg, poppy seeds) exactly as they were a half millennium ago. Potato gnocchi, on the other hand, have accepted tomatoes, which could not be otherwise: Two American products have come together again in a European recipe.

What shape do gnocchi take? If their nature is simply that of being a piece of dough, a piece of something, esthetics have little to do with it. However, their shapes are numerous: small and large, wide and narrow, oval, oblong, cylindrical, spherical, cubed. . . . As always, fantasy and imagination have added flavor to the dish, along with the stimulus of a hungry stomach. The dream of the Land of Bengodì is not only of hunger satiated but also of the pleasure of eating—a pleasure in which shapes also play a major role.

The patient took some broth

The old adage, "The patient[5] took some broth," attributing restorative virtues to the concentration of meat juices served hot (the

---

[5] Or sick person.

Spanish word for broth is simply "hot," caldo), would seem to exclude any question of taste in this kind of preparation. The nutritional aspect is predominant, the idea of efficacy overriding tastiness. Broth—with all its technical and conceptual variations, such as clear, with small pasta or rice, vegetables, and so on—historically belongs to the tradition of subsistence. The peasant tradition, in particular, has entrusted to the pot and to its long simmering the task of restoring the body exhausted by labor, extracting to the last drop the nutritional benefits of meat and vegetables. The model of home cooking, by definition, is that of the cauldron over an ever-lit fire: much preparation but unhurried, a great deal of patience, and the serenity of a dish that does not leave room for inventiveness.

Everything went into that broth, and I have often wondered if that is related to a singular coincidence of terminology seen in Romance languages: *Jus* meant broth to the ancient Romans, the juice or sap of foods (the French *jus* is still active). At the same time *jus* meant the body of laws, the concentration of knowledge and norms that regulated human relations. A new term, *brodium,* circulated during the Middle Ages, apparently derived from Old German, as did *suppa.* A coincidence perhaps, but it is a fact that along with the Latin legacy, the German models are evident and important in medieval cooking: Broths and soups were widely eaten (and are seen still today in the culinary habits of Eastern Europe).

Broth for ordinary days, in short, whereas in the traditions of peasant society, the joy of a holiday was celebrated instead with the fragrance of a roast or the sizzling of frying food. Even broth can be festive when the scent is no longer vague, the piece of meat in it is choicer, the flavor is clearer and stronger. On important days other delicacies are cooked in that broth: small stuffed shapes, tasty rounds of dough carefully molded. Cappelletti, tortellini, agnolini, passatelli rise to great heights in the flavorful broth: It is Sunday.

Exiled from their historical ally of broth, served dried instead with added condiments, those marvels of gastronomic fantasy change radically. Today it is increasingly rare to find them floating in broth, because broth is incompatible with speed or experimentation: the two pillars of present-day restaurant cooking, which looks at fast food with one eye and at creative cuisine with the other. Broth is home food, and the disappearance of broth comes from the decline in home cooking. Will the tradition of broth manage to survive? Or must we be satisfied with "portable broth," that ingenious invention of Justus von Liebig, who, in the nineteenth century, invented a magic tablet for the rapid reconstitution of the taste of broth, even outside the home? Will it redeem the pitiful broth made in hospitals, which in form would seem to evoke ancient wisdom ("the patient took some broth"), but in substance reduces that broth to nothing, deprived of flavor and comfort, in an anti-cooking kitchen that looks bitterly penitential.

The patient is entitled to good broth.

The invention of fried potatoes

In the history of culinary practices, the acceptance of new products in many cases is favored by processes of adaptation and assimilation. "The reduction of the unknown to the known," as it is termed by anthropologists.

When corn arrived in Europe from America it was used almost exclusively as polenta, a traditional European dish (prepared in ancient Rome with spelt, in the Middle Ages with millet and other grains) unknown in America. The potato also underwent various attempts at reinterpretation. For example, it was used to make bread, reduced to a mash, and added to wheat flour in an attempt to produce the most traditional and characteristic food of the European diet. This idea was proposed by such eighteenth-century intellectuals as the French agronomist Antoine Parmentier, or in Italy by Giovanni Battara. The idea of making bread with potatoes had no sequel, because the starch does not rise. Nonetheless, this attempt has great cultural significance because it demonstrates the will to "bend" innovations to tradition.

Much more successful was the use of potatoes in making gnocchi, a dish much loved by Europeans as of the Middle Ages, until then made entirely with flour and bread crumbs. The real triumph, however, was the invention of fried potatoes.

Frying was a way of cooking that was typically, though not exclusively, European, much appreciated in popular but also in upper-class cuisine. Ever since the Middle Ages particular attention was paid to techniques of frying (in oil, butter, or lard, according to local availability and liturgical seasons) in the preparation of many gastronomic specialties, both savory and sweet, in some cases related to holidays and special recurring events. Frying was unknown to the traditional cuisines of America, where there was no oil, butter, or lard. Olives, cows, and hogs were taken across the ocean by European conquistadors.

Fried potatoes are therefore a perfect metaphor for what happens in culinary history when diverse cultures meet, are compared, and blend. The product is new, coming from outside or from far away. The method of dealing with it is ancient and has deep roots in the host culture. We can then discuss the priorities: Anglo-Saxons across the ocean call fried potatoes *French* fries (except when contesting the attribution at a time of political tension with France), but Belgians have no doubt that French paternity is a fraud and that real fried potatoes, *frites*, should be fried not once but twice, as only they do. We will have to agree on what is meant by frying: deep frying or sautéing in a pan, or coating with oil and roasting. As many domestic traditions teach, these are only variations of a single practice, a distinctive practice of European cooking. Even in this case, it has succeeded in exporting to the world and imposing on the world its own model. A history, among others, of gastronomic imperialism.

Among the thousand ways to prepare eggs

Fried eggs, scrambled eggs, poached, hard-boiled, raked in embers, left on the hearth, deviled. . . . These are only a few of the ways eggs can be prepared, and then in sacrifice to the Belly god, on fast days, "infralardellati," slipped between two strips of lard. We read this in the fourth book of Gargantua and Pantagruel, in which François Rabelais dreamed up lists of delicacies permitted during periods of abstinence from meat: dishes and products whose destiny within the culinary traditions of Europe is also tied to this identity of substitution of the prohibited food.

As of the Middle Ages, this privilege concerned such foods as fish, cheese, and, of course, eggs. The way medieval monks succeeded in observing the obligation of abstinence, without, however, denying themselves the pleasures of the palate, is revealed with great vivacity in a twelfth-century polemical text by Saint Bernard, abbot of Clairvaux and founder of the Cistercian order, who, reproaching his adversaries at the monastery of Cluny for their excessive attention to gastronomy, took as an example eggs and the extraordinary, improper in his view, variety of ways they were prepared in the kitchens of the Burgundian monastery: "Who can say in how many ways eggs are poured and scrambled, with how much skill they are flipped and reflipped, liquefied, hardened, crumbled, brought to the table now fried, now roasted, now stuffed, now accompanied by other foods, now by themselves?"

Cookbooks of the Middle Ages and even later also gave ample space to eggs. Entire chapters are devoted to illustrating some of the infinite uses of this product, presumed to be humble and simple, which one can scarcely do without in the process of preparing food. Platina, the fifteenth-century humanist, reproducing recipes already present in the cookbook of Maestro Martino, his favorite cook, spends much time on the innumerable ways of making fritters, and then goes on to recipes for making eggs: fried, scrambled, boiled, divided (hard-boiled and cut in half), on the grill, in a torte, in a pan "*alla fiorentina*" (with spinach)." Particularly virtuosic is the preparation of eggs "on a spit," in the middle of a fireplace, which we see in a miniature of his *Tacuinum sanitatis.* In truth, Platina does not seem too convinced. Eggs on a spit, he writes, "are a senseless invention, a bizarre idea or the joke of certain cooks."

If these "inventions" fall into the category of culinary snobbism, the importance of eggs in the Middle Ages and still today remains a fact shared by all social groups. Landowners always required the annual tribute of some eggs, by way of "obligatory homage" because peasants were not short on eggs. They were a basic resource in the peasant diet, which for centuries practiced abstinence from meat—not out of liturgical observance but out of necessity—and thus knew (or had to know) the value of alternative products. A Tuscan cookbook of the fourteenth century gives us an idea of this vast world of consumers, this socially diffused competence, when it laconically states, "as to eggs, fried, roasted and scrambled, it is so well known there is no need for any mention."

Fritters

"Whatever can be fried is good to eat," assures a proverb common in various regions of Italy. This may be why fritters[6] take their name not from their ingredients but from the simple fact of being fried, fritte. As Platina explains, frictelle (a new term unknown to the ancients) is derived from fricto, because "this type of dish is cooked by frying." This is an obviousness that borders on tautology.

The first Italian cookbooks, which go back to the Middle Ages, distinguish between Lenten and non-Lenten fritters. The first are fried in oil (the fat typical of Lent and fast days during which animal products are prohibited); the second, in lard (the fat typical of "normal" days). A Tuscan cookbook of the fourteenth century, based on an earlier model from southern Italy, gives us the recipe for *dulcimane* (extremely simple fritters made only of flour, water, and eggs, sweetened with honey) while considering both possibilities: "Take flour mixed with water and eggs, roll thin and stretch; cut it in the shape of leaves, or figs, or whatever you like,

---

[6] *Fritelle* in Italian.

and *fry them in lard or oil* to cover; once cooked, spread some boiled honey on top and eat." Lard or oil; what matters is the depth. Only in this way can fritters be crunchy and tasty, and paradoxically, less greasy, as well we know. If immersed completely in fat, the cooking time is reduced and with it the amount of fat absorbed.

Maestro Martino, that celebrated fifteenth-century cook, devoted an entire chapter of his book on the art of cooking to fritters, explaining in abundant detail how "to make each *frictella*": of elder tree flowers, of egg white with fine flour and fresh cheese, of clotted milk, of sage, of apples, of bay leaves, of almonds, with every kind of fat: "If it is during the Lenten season, you can fry them in oil, and do not add animal fat or eggs."

In short, whether Carnival or Lent, Sunday or Friday, hot or cold, raining or bright, we will not be short of fritters. Fried food is not seasonal; it can be paired with any meteorological, social, or liturgical condition. It is not by chance that the four *tempora* of the Christian liturgy—the periods of abstinence that marked the annual passage of the seasons—gave their name to a particular type of fried food: *tempura*, which came to Japan from Europe.

The flavor of fried food and of fritters was and is different each time, determined in some instances by the persuasive intensity of lard, in others by the soft sweetness of butter (which was gradually accepted during the Middle Ages as a fast-day alternative to oil, in still others by the slightly bitter acidity of olive oil (on which modern dietary science is conferring increasing importance). Religious and scientific motivations have confused and superimposed themselves on simple reasons of taste, economy, and tradition, so clearly recalled by Pellegrino Artusi when he wrote in his *Science in the Kitchen* (1891): "People use for frying the fat that they produce best in their own region: In Tuscany preference is given to olive oil; in Lombardy, to butter; and in Emilia, to lard."

A well-made fritter is pleasurable to all the senses. Its aroma invites us to taste it. The golden color of its crust is pleasing to the eye, the bubbling of the fat on its surface delights the ear, and the sense of touch is gratified by a food that is at its best when brought to the mouth with one's fingers.

Don't flip the frittata

"Who does not know how to make a frittata? And who in this world has not at some time in his life made some kind of frittata?"

This is how Pellegrino Artusi opens his famous cookbook, the foundation of domestic cooking in Italy (recipe no.145, Various *frittate*). "Still," he continues, "it would not be entirely superfluous to say a few words on the subject." Even the simplest things (most of all, the simplest things) have to be well made with the care and attention they deserve, and with the respect owed to the "fundamentals"—as an economist would say—of daily life. To continue with Artusi: "The eggs for a frittata should not be overbeaten: mix them in a bowl with a fork, and when you see the whites blended with the yolks, stop." To cook a frittata, he recommends "that excellent Tuscan oil," and the first rule is never to flip it. A frittata "is cooked on one side only, which is always the preferred way of doing it. . . . When the underside is solid, the pan is turned over a plate held in the other hand, and one goes to the table."

From this (it may be said parenthetically) comes the metaphor "*girare la frittata*," to flip the frittata, meaning to change one's tune, to turn the situation to one's advantage, which is not only ethically reprehensible, but also gastronomically incorrect.

The Artusian model (no longer accepted today, to the point that a frittata can now be equated with an omelet, precisely because it is cooked on both sides) boasted an old tradition. It was already proposed in the fifteenth century by Maestro Martino in the chapter on eggs in his *Libro de arte coquinaria* (*Book on the Art of Cooking*). The *frictata*, with which the chapter begins, is supposed to be made in this way: "Beat the eggs thoroughly, add a little water and a little milk to make it soft, along with some good grated cheese." As for fat, Martino, a Lombard, prefers butter: Cook it, he writes, "in good butter because that is fatter." Note the positive connotation of the notion of "fat" then as opposed to today. Martino continues: "To make it properly it should not be turned or cooked too long." Just like Artusi.

To make a good frittata is a recognized talent, the subject of one of the entertaining stories in *Facezie*[7] of a fifteenth-century Tuscan writer. "What shall we eat for dinner tonight, since it is Friday?" ask the gentlemen gathered in the palace of Giovanni de' Medici in Fiesole. They finally decide to have the cook make eggs, prepared in various styles. When the dishes arrive, Giovanni reproaches the cook: "It seems to me that you have forgotten how to cook. Look at the frittate[8] you sent us." The cook tries to exculpate himself by blaming the pan, protesting that, "It does not do a good job." "Go make some others," the master tells him, "and dedicate them to Saint Cresci to make them come out properly." Useless, they were worse than before. A few days later, the gentlemen ran into Arlotto, the priest of the parish church of S. Cresci, and complained that they had not received the grace of the saint. The priest responded with irritation: "Are you not ashamed to have so little respect for my good Saint Cresci? He behaved in the manner you deserved. Do you really think he is the saint of frittate?" Which is to say, leave the saints alone. To make a good frittata, all you need is a cook, provided he's good at it.

Sausages

The sausage, in all its varieties, including frankfurters, is as ancient as the pig. Cicero, recalling a saying of Crisippus, wrote that salt for the pig is a little like the soul: The latter keeps it alive, the former preserves its meat. The pig was used by humans as a kind of pantry, a protection against the risk of famine, on condition of

---

[7] Pranks.
[8] Plural of *frittata*.

salting it and seasoning it well, putting to use the extraordinary durability, moisture, and abundant fat of its meat.

This is why the sausage,[9] like all cured meat [*salumeria*], takes its name from salt [*sale*], rather than its constituent ingredients. Even the word *würstel* refers not to the contents (stuffings can be extremely varied) but to the method of making it, preparing it, seasoning it: The root is analogous to *würzen,* which indicates the herbs, spices, condiments used.

The history of eating (which coincides at least in part with the history of hunger) owes a great deal to these little "stuffed bags." Raw, like many sausages, or cooked, as frankfurters and the like usually are, sliced or heated, accompanied by bread or placed inside a bun, these ingenious creations have for centuries aided in the human fight for survival. They also occupy an important place in the history of gastronomy, the fraternal companion (fortunately) of the history of hunger. As a result, we have the display of sausages that appears in the markets, each with its attribute of regional specialty, delicacies that reveal the invention of human beings, their amazing ability to translate need into pleasure.

Ortensio Lando, that strange Milanese scholar, forerunner of gastronomic tourism, imagined in 1548 a tour of Italy from Sicily to the Alps to savor at every stop the local specialties. Among pastas and fish, wines and cheeses, cakes and marzipan, special attention was given to cured and salted meats, and particularly to sausages. The highest praise went to Bologna, where "the best sausages ever eaten are made: whether raw or cooked, they whet the appetite at any hour and enhance the wine, even if it has gone bad and lost its flavor." Therefore, "I bless whoever invented them, I kiss and adore the ingenious hands that fashioned them." In Modena as well "you will have good sausages," and in Lucca, "oh, what a delicious sausage!" Lando then addresses an imaginary foreign traveler visiting Italy: "Nor should you overlook the slender luganica and tomacelle of Monza" (other sausage names of medieval memory).

---

[9] *Salsiccia* in Italian.

Sausages primarily made of the brains and blood of pigs are the "cervelati"[10] of Milan, "monarch among foods," accompanied by good "offellette" and cool vernaccia.[11]

The preparation of sausages, when made at home, was entrusted to sausage makers, quite different from cooks. Cooks themselves dealt with sausages, because they were often used in dishes. For example, we find them in the monumental treatise by Bartolomeo Scappi (1570), the most outstanding cook of the Renaissance: "*Li salsiccioni*,[12] to be good, must be made of young pork, and from loins of young steer, and should be slightly salty and firm." They can be stored for months in olive oil, turned from time to time, and kept "in a place not too warm or airy."

In their diversity, which nonetheless goes back to a perfectly recognizable genre, sausages amply demonstrate the idea of variety in unity—typical of the tradition of Italian gastronomy.

Pink pigs, black pigs

Once upon a time pigs were very different from what they are today. During the Middle Ages they were raised in the open in woods; they ran freely and were therefore lean and slender, somewhat like boar, with which they had frequent contact, even couplings on occasion. There was great similarity between the domestic and the wild species because their way of life and their food habits were so similar (acorns, the nuts of beech trees, berries). The difference in the pigs of today does not depend on that alone. The breeds are different from those that were common in past centuries.

In medieval miniatures and frescoes one can see the principal characteristics of those pigs when compared with present-day

---

[10] From *cervello*, brain.

[11] A white wine from central–northern Italy.

[12] Thick sausages.

breeds: larger and longer head; pointed snout, rather than flat; short, erect ears; stiff hairs on the back; visible canines. A far cry from the pink piglets to which Walt Disney accustomed us. Premodern animals were for the most part dark in color, red to blackish. Vincenzo Tanara, a Bolognese agronomist of the seventeenth century, assures us that the best kind are the red, "delicate to eat," whereas the black variety had the advantage of being "solid meat, and longer lasting than the other." Pale-skinned pigs were not much appreciated. A type of pig typical of the Middle Ages and still known today, though scarce, is the *cintato* or *cinto senese* (not only in the region of Siena but also in Sardinia and elsewhere), identified by a large white stripe down the center of a black body. It can be seen in the fresco of Good Government by Ambrogio Lorenzetti in the municipal palace of Siena.

All of these breeds were smaller than those of today, because they were not forcibly fattened, except for a short period just before slaughter. During the Middle Ages their weight could go from a minimum of 30–40 kilos to a maximum of 70–80, approximately a third of the weights common today.

Even if the pink pig of northern European origin is uncontested in intensive pig-raising today, the history of "medieval" pigs does not seem to have ended. Passionate archaeologist-breeders can be found who persist in keeping the breed alive. Marco, on the Tuscan-Romagnolo Apennines, has for a number of years raised in his woods a handsome little herd of *cintoni* quite similar to those in medieval miniatures. Because he found some differences (for example, his pigs did not have the elongated snout of those of a millennium ago), he crossed them with dark boars in the hope of restoring the wild genes. After a few generations, this "regressive selection" brought his pigs back to their ancient appearance (and perhaps to their ancient flavor). Here is an instance of the conservation of a cultural heritage that is worth noting as a possible means of reviving our pastoral economy and perhaps of rediscovering the flavors that we too hastily tossed away.

Liberating vegetarian cooking

Vegetarian restaurants are multiplying, and the demand for alternative foods to meat continues to grow. Motivations vary, as do the attitudes that preceded this choice. To choose a vegetarian diet, of whatever rigor, can indicate respect for animals, whether out of commitment to precise ideologies or philosophies, or, more commonly, out of sympathy, out of discomfort with the thought that our food depends on eliminating a life. In other cases, ecological considerations prevail: the awareness that animal farming consumes much more energy than vegetable farming, and is therefore more harmful to the environment. When it comes to respect for animals or the environment, more subjective considerations can become involved related to personal health and the conviction that a vegetarian diet is more salutary. Nor is there a lack of reasons based on pleasure: Vegetable cuisine is inventive, varied, and tasty. Then there is, as always, the matter of trendiness. Whatever the motives, the number of consumers who prefer not to eat meat is increasing.

It is nonetheless curious that in many cases vegetarian cooking is lacking in autonomous gastronomy. Vegetarian dishes often are "faked" to look like—if only in name—a traditional meat dish, as though there were a reluctance to abandon meat entirely. An article in *Sole 24 Ore* of January 27, 2007, describes the menus of a growing number of restaurants that are opening in China to satisfy the demands of a clientele committed to a culture like Buddhism, traditionally averse to eating animals.

These menus contain roast chicken or sweet and sour pork, lacquered duck and fried eel: Meat dishes typical of Chinese cuisine reappear, in form if not in substance, made with vegetable products that imitate to perfection their traditional models. Products such as tofu, which are extremely malleable, are subjected to remarkable manipulations that transform them into legs, wings, breasts of poultry.

Less commonly and less systematically, even in the West one can find vegetable sausages, soy steaks, and all kinds of substitute foods that simulate dishes of very different origins. This kind of cuisine seems highly contradictory. Although it proclaims the desire to detach itself from the carnivorous model, in reality it continues to imitate it and thus confirms it as the reigning model. A genuine vegetarian cuisine will be one that eventually succeeds in emancipating itself by affirming its own separate identity.

Dressing a salad

Even the tender salad has a history, and it too has had its bards. One of them was the physician and botanist Costanzo Felici from Piobbico, in the Marches. Around 1570, he wrote a very lengthy "Letter on salad greens and plants that in some way enter the human diet." It is a veritable treatise, part botanical, part dietary, part gastronomic. Hundreds of plants are taken into account with minute attention to the method of cultivating them in vegetable gardens or gathering them in fields, the beneficent properties they can transmit to humans, the best way to prepare them and eat them.

This letter/treatise on salad greens was addressed by Felici to his mentor Ulisse Aldrovandi, the great Bolognese naturalist, not only as a matter of scientific curiosity, but also out of more personal interest: "You," the author writes to his teacher, "who so much enjoy the food of salads." He added that Italians are generally "so avid" about salads that they are mocked by foreigners, who see this habit of eating raw greens as "depriving grazing animals of their food." This joking polemic demonstrates that Italian alimentary taste even then had a well-defined and clearly recognizable character.

How, Felici wonders, did salad get its name? For the reason, he replies, that it is never eaten without salt, or without vinegar. The Romans called it *acetaria*,[13] Strangely, however, no reference was

---

[13] *Aceto* is the word for vinegar in modern Italian, from the Latin *acetum*.

ever made to oil, the third condiment essential to a good salad, as shown in the Italian proverb *insalata ben salata, poco aceto e ben oliata* (salad well salted, little vinegar and well oiled). The reason, Felici explains, is perhaps that salt and vinegar are absolutely necessary "to dry the tasteless moisture of the greens," to prevent them from rotting and to make them more pleasing to the taste. Oil is added not out of necessity but only to enhance the dish, to please the demands of the palate. Moreover, there are other practices, such as adding "syrup, honey or sugar, or the like."

When should salad be eaten? Felici says its uses are infinite: There are those who prefer it at lunch and those who prefer it at dinner; at the beginning of the meal, or at the end. His opinion, supported by learned citations of ancient writers, is that it is preferable to eat it at the beginning, since its acidity "sharpens and stimulates the appetite," predisposing the stomach to assimilate and to digest food. Gluttons are well aware of this and have salad served midway during the meal to "revive the appetite already lost," meaning to reawaken the desire to eat. These are habits Felici does not condone, because "eating too much stretches the skin." Moreover, "Every excess is a vice."

The blender and the mortar

The mortar is the blender of premodern kitchens. Whereas we tend today to make judicious use of the blender, for the cook of the Middle Ages and the Renaissance the mortar was the principal device and totally indispensable for day-to-day preparations. This was due to the gastronomic centrality of sauces that were held, in those days, to be the requisite accompaniment of every dish, the necessary "corrective" (in an almost pharmaceutical sense) of meat, fish, or any food served. Added to this was a different perception of the cook's relation to his raw material. Meat, fish, and vegetables are seen today (by many, if not by all) as products whose "natural" identity is to be respected, which allows them to be fully appreciated for taste, nutrition, and esthetics. Centuries ago, instead, the natural product was not particularly valued; on the contrary, it was thought almost the duty of the cook to modify its flavor, color, and texture radically. To crush basil or marjoram, or the costly spices of the Orient, was the initial operation in preparing every sauce and condiment. Even meat, fish, vegetables, and cheese were reduced, altered, and recomposed into tortes, molds, "artificial" compositions that changed their distinguishing characteristics to the point of disappearance.

Let us take as an example the most ancient of Italian cookbooks, the *Liber de coquina*, written at the beginning of the fourteenth century at the Angevine court in Naples. The presence of the mortar and pestle on the work table is constant, inescapable. The direction to "*pestare*," grind, or "*tritare*," mince, recurs in all the recipes. Herbs are ground to reduce them to a paste: "Take parsley, dill, marjoram, fennel, onion, spices along with saffron. Grind all of it well in a mortar. Cook with oil and serve." Vegetables are ground: "Cook peas and remove their shells. When you have ground them finely in a pot or in a mortar, add lard, pour them into a bowl and let them cool, that way they thicken." Broad beans, once boiled, are to be "ground in a mortar." Lentils, cooked with fragrant herbs, should be "well ground." The same is true in the preparation of broths and soups: always grind, grind, grind. Fish can also be prepared this way: "Shell chick peas and cook them with fish that has been sliced or pounded and ground in the mortar." By grinding meat, one can make delicious *pasticci*,[14] and if egg yolks enter into the mixture, it is understood that they too will be cooked and mashed. Herbs, spices, bread crumbs, liver, all of them ground, will give flavor to braised meat. A dish and its sauce will be united under the sign of the mortar, the pestle, and their faithful companion the strainer, to make the mixture more homogeneous.

---

[14] Baked layered dishes.

With time, utensils multiplied and improved. In the Renaissance kitchen of Bartolomeo Scappi, equipped with every kind of device, the mortar was always at the center of operations. This great cook (who worked at the papal court) requested among his other equipment "large and small bronze mortars with their pestles for grinding spices," and "mortars of marble and other stone with their pestles of hard wood," along with colanders and "strainers, large and small."

Mediterranean "fusion"

Fusion cuisine and the Mediterranean diet would seem to be antagonistic: a cuisine of mixture, hybridization, impurity versus the gastronomic identity (the product of ancient wisdom, of an intimate relation with the land) of the civilizations that evolved around the Mediterranean. This was not exactly the major concern of the scholars who assembled in February 2004 in Barcelona for a colloquium devoted to "Flavors of the Mediterranean." Among the many topics, one emerged with particular salience: The Mediterranean is a geographic reality endowed with common elements, determined by climate and topography, but on the basis of this common foundation, diverse cultures, languages, and traditions (including culinary) arose. What has historically characterized the Mediterranean has been its natural tendency (favored by the short distances from east to west and north to south) to develop as a common zone of exchange among people, products, and culture. Mediterranean identity exists precisely and entirely within that exchange, that coming together of "natural" differences, born of history rather than of geography.

The name *mare nostrum*, our sea, that the Romans gave the Mediterranean expressed not only an imperial strategy but also a cultural unity. During the Middle Ages this common framework was severely threatened by the Islamic occupation of Africa (as well as parts of Sicily and Spain), which transformed the Mediterranean from an "interior lake" into a sea of borders that separated two worlds with differing values, including food. And yet, these same Arabs were the promoters of a new synthesis through their exportation of products and flavors until then unknown in the West (citrus fruits, sugar, eggplants, artichokes, rice, dried pasta, new spices), which gave rise to a renewed Mediterranean identity that brought together Islamic and Christian regions. An example is the predominant taste for sweetness, typical of the Islamic tradition, that became entrenched in southern Europe. In the Modern Era the arrival of products from the Americas (tomatoes and potatoes, sweet and hot peppers, corn) again altered Mediterranean identity.

What today we are accustomed to call, too simplistically, the "Mediterranean diet" is an abstraction that corresponds only in part to this history. It is a model theoretically constructed, beginning in the 1950s, for very precise medical and health reasons: to find a corrective to the diet of wealthy nations that is excessively high in proteins and calories ,with America in first place. This is a model we Mediterraneans can also share, on condition that we do not reduce it to a nutritional regimen, that we do not mummify it into a hygienic prescription. The lesson that history teaches is that we regard this alimentary system not as a simple reality, dictated by the "nature" of localities, but rather as a complex construction tied to a culture, to a way of life that Mediterranean peoples learned to share, to modify, to create day by day.

Home cooking: when variation is the rule

It is easy to say "home cooking." It is easy to wish that it be appreciated, preserved, handed down. In the meantime, where do we find it? In the home, one would say. Today, however, home has become the ideal market for industrial cooking, the center of the tendency toward cultural homogeneity and the loss of local differences, assailed by publicity and a work timetable that leaves increasingly less time for the traditional methods of domestic cooking. Paradoxically, in many homes it is restaurant food that has assumed the role of providing a revival of home cooking, a heritage dear to all, forgotten by many. We must retrieve this heritage. We must look around without prejudice, observe widely, collect documentation wherever possible, inside the home obviously, but also outside.

The problem will then be to determine the right way to describe this kind of "home cooking"—not to codify it, as some people claim to do, because what best characterizes any oral tradition is variation, the individual's detachment from the norm. This obviously does not deny (on the contrary, it implies) that a norm exists, but without the "authoritative" character that distinguishes professional cooking, identifiable precisely in codified and codifiable rules. Home cooking, on the contrary, operates in a multitude of possible alternatives that direct the preparation of food on a daily basis: Recipes vary from one country to another, from one family to another, and the variations, far from being shared, assume a distinctly identifying quality that is often expressed in the suggestive framework of "secrecy."

Home cooking can therefore not be codified; it can only be described, in a simple way or, better yet, a simplified way. The basic techniques and procedures can be determined, as well as the minimal common denominator that holds together the individual preparations (the typology of individual preparations) with their principal variations, taking into account the ways ingredients are used and how they are prepared, here too within the limitations of fundamental alternatives. This makes it possible to determine the essential factors on which the identity of home cooking was founded: economy, practicality, function, relation to the territory (and the market). These are principles that, deduced from the analysis of specific situations, can become an interpretive model without predetermined confines. "Home cooking" is not just in *our* home, but the cooking in all homes, wherever communities of families gather around a table. Home cooking lives everywhere.

Cooking is home

Certain dialectical expressions identify the home with the kitchen. In Romagna, for example, *andé in cà*, to go home, means *andare in cucina*, to go to the kitchen. This comes from the centrality, not merely metaphoric but actual, physical, that the kitchen has always had in peasant homes. A single room, a grate with a fire in the middle and in some cases an opening above it to let out the smoke, welcomed whoever came in. One gathered around the fire for warmth, one cooked food on it, one ate there. This was the heart of the house.

In upper-class dwellings, however, the kitchen was kept as far from the living areas as possible. In patrician palaces the kitchen was often found on a different floor from the dining room, as though to conceal the "base" work of the cooks from the view of guests—even in the case of extraordinary kitchens, hypertechnological, like the one described by Bartolomeo Scappi, the cook of Pope Pius V, in his famous treatise on cooking of 1570.

Scappi's kitchen, an ideal kitchen, meticulously illustrated in a series of engravings at the back of the book, included a principal room with stoves, ovens, tables, shelves, basins, and mortars; another room with all the utensils for making pasta, sauces, and "many other dishes"; a courtyard with a well and a sink, intended for the cleaning of meat, fish, and vegetables; a pantry for keeping meat cool; and another pantry for storing utensils and implements. For the use of the personnel there was surely a changing room and a nook where they ate.

All this, Scappi warns, should be consigned "preferably to a location far from the public . . . so as not to bother the nearby rooms of the palace with the noise that is necessarily made." The kitchen must remain hidden.

Between two such different concepts of a kitchen—a kitchen so central as to become synonymous with house and a kitchen that is to be concealed and separated from the "important" parts of the house—it is the first, the popular, peasant one, that ended up as the kitchen of choice after centuries of cultural inferiority. This took place during the twentieth century with the growing scarcity of domestic help in middle-class homes and the demands of the lady of the house, now obliged to work in the kitchen, not to be excluded from the conversation in the living and dining rooms. This is how the kitchen–dining room came into being in the 1930s, "a modern formula appreciated by architects and clients alike," as described in an article in *Mode pratique* of April 1934. The new idea of a room with multiple functions, called *cucina all'americana*, American-style kitchen, met with great success after World War II. It is a new idea, yet an old one. The kitchen–living room, the "livable" kitchen, is in a way the retrieval by bourgeois culture of the traditional peasant model of the kitchen–house, a model contrary to the patrician idea of separation.

In these last decades the kitchen has acquired even more space within the house. Someone, for reasons of space, tried to reduce it to a cooking area, but this very simplification only affirmed its presence in crucial areas of domestic life. The kitchen has reclaimed its centrality, and often obtains it. To design a house around the kitchen is no longer a mark of poverty but a project that inspires the ingenuity of trendy architects. The kitchen no longer has to hide; on the contrary, it can show off.

This can also be seen in fashionable restaurants, where the so-called open kitchen proudly displays the work of the chef, no longer relegated to hidden recesses. Now the highest privilege is to get a table right next to the kitchen.

FOUR

The Gastronomy of Hunger

Nameless plants

"At the end of winter and the beginning of spring it was said prover-bially among women that every green plant goes into a salad." This was written, around 1570, by Costanzo Felici in his treatise "On Salads and Plants That in Some Way Become Food for Humans," addressed to his teacher, the famous botanist Ulisse Aldrovandi, professor of natural sciences at the University of Bologna.

The passage quoted above is the introduction to a long descrip-tion of particular interest because it allows us to open an essential chapter on the history of food that always runs the risk of disap-pearing from the written documentation on which the historian bases his work, namely, a knowledge of the land and the plants it generates spontaneously, and the oral transmission of knowledge shared by common people, recognized as extremely important even by official science (as indicated by the attention Felici gives it). A fine thread ties the academic works of Aldrovandi—who studies and draws the plants in his herbarium—to the daily practices of the women who scour the fields in search of "green herbs" and always find new ones for their salads, "because they mix into them many plants without names or scarcely used." Just that: *plants without names.* Felici seems to be admitting that peasant women gather plants whose existence even university professors ignore.

Women: Even this is an important admission. Felici attributes a privileged familiarity, a special relationship with food born of their intimacy with the earth and its products. It is through comments like these that a treatise on botany can open unexpected windows of anthropological thinking.

Which herbs go into these end-of-winter "mixtures"? Felici's women (he is referring to the customs of his region, between Rimini and the Marches) "gather among the vines a kind of wild lettuce, which they call fat herb, that has bitter leaves spotted with white, and yellow bell-shaped flowers . . . they also call it 'fat hen' and 'wolf's testicles'"; and "the whole rib of young scabiosa"; as well as many other herbs and flowers also good in salads; and "a tiny branched creeping herb, with little yellow flowers and small leaflets like three-leaf field clover" that they call "hare's ear." (Felici often lists the popular names of plants, comparing them with the scientific names.) He lists and describes dozens of plants "and I have heard of many others which I no longer remember."

To remember them all is practically impossible, as it is impossible to catalogue the diversity of foods that went into those salads "according to their fantasy." These are fantasies that sustain the daily diet and are doubly useful in times of famine, "because at such times one gathers everything, and everything, they say, fills the stomach." Hunger stimulates ingenuity, every resource is put to use.

How many of us would still know how to do that?

Field herbs

If someone says "field herbs" you think of ditches, meadows, spontaneous vegetation. You think of a food created by nature, not by man. You think of plants that during the cold season (and beyond, all the way to spring) cheer the table with various flavors, wilder, more bitter, at times tastier. You think of the herbs that provide us with infusions for a sore throat and cold winter afternoons. Medieval monks called it Providence and assigned many alimentary needs to it, without forgetting that the largest share of such provisions came from Work.

This is the ancient dialectic between nature and culture that recurs in the domain of food. Produce our own food or wait for Someone to take care of us? Count on the generosity of God, climate, soil, or roll up our sleeves to earn our daily bread with the hoe and the spade? Some (like Saint Benedict) upheld the first option, celebrating the value of fatigue and labor. Others preferred to isolate themselves from the world, become hermits in wooded solitude, and rely on Providence (or alms) for their survival. Most played both sides. They cultivated the land, the fields, the orchards, but at the same time assisted nature's signals. They learned how to recognize plants, how to distinguish edible plants from poisonous ones, how to care for a vegetable heritage that was useful "both to feed us and to keep us in good health," as the monk Cassiodoro wrote in the sixth century. The vegetable gardens and orchards of the Middle Ages (cultivated by monks, assuredly, but also those of nobles and peasants) were extraordinary sites of experimentation where a knowledge of agronomy and farming practices blended with a knowledge of wild plants. Much of the alimentary and gastronomic culture of our past emerged from these two kinds of knowledge.

This is why we speak of *field* (a word that evokes agricultural labor, the cultivation of the land) even when we mean meadows or ditches in which wild herbs grow. This can happen because a millennial culture has taught us not to raise rigid barriers between the two worlds. The domestic is more productive, more reassuring, gentler than the wild, but when joined to the wild it becomes complete and tastes better; moreover, whatever is domestic has wild roots. It is fortunate in the case of cardoons and fennel that the genius of farmers and horticulturists was able to transform them into sweet, succulent vegetables; but the bitter aftertaste of the cardoon and its graceless shape are the mark (much appreciated by gastronomes: "the uglier, the tastier") of untamed wildness. The intractable fennel, which no wine can accompany, demonstrates a nature only partly domesticated. As for radicchio, mallow, borage, beet greens, chicory, we must admit that domestic and wild species are not mutually exclusive; on the contrary, they complement each other. As the botanist Felici wrote in the sixteenth century, "Chicory or sunflower or radicchio . . . are plants much appreciated in the salads of every season, thus the cultivated . . . like the wild."

Bitter and sweet go well together.

Forgotten fruits, or rediscovered?

There is often a confusion between history and memory, as though they were one and the same. Not so, as Jacques Le Goff taught us in a well-known essay. Memory is short and selective. It only recalls the most recent events or those that for whatever reason we chose to extract from the pile. Memory is not a receptacle of what happened; it is an ability, a mental organ, a function that tends to atrophy if not used constantly. Moreover, memory deforms. What we believe it remembers is not the truth, but an image we have made of it. It is for this that the work of a historian is useful: to stitch together the fragments of a distracted memory, to verify them, confront them with the traces carried over by the past. Those traces are within us, one has only to look to find them. Then we become aware that what seemed to be lost, in reality was only forgotten and was worth the effort to recall because the best of all possible worlds is not our own, nor that of a hundred or a thousand years ago, but the one that succeeds in treasuring the best that all worlds possess.

Even a fruit can serve this purpose: a medlar, a jujube, an arbutus, a vulpine pear. If we have relegated them to a dark corner of our memory, because other things, more important, more urgent, weighed on us, it would not be pointless to recapture their flavor.

These forgotten fruits were not the great protagonists of history. Even the quince, the sorb, the cornel, the crab apple, can be turned into marmalade or jam, but that is clearly not the way to remedy the cramp of hunger. However, their function was precisely to introduce something unusual, different, strange into the monotony of life and the daily diet, which has always been essential to good living. A taste for the superfluous and enjoyment of what is beautiful (and good) are not strictly limited to the well-to-do. Tribal societies consider certain useless objects necessary because their sole, and extremely important, function is to keep the spirit happy. If the spirit is bored, it will leave the body, and without the spirit there is no survival.

It has happened that certain things fell into oblivion simply because they were useless. Let us go back to our fruits. Their yield is small, they are neither big nor beautiful, they do not keep, they are even somewhat sour. Above all, they are not profitable: a mortal sin in a consumer society. Those fruits are not lost, merely forgotten. If reviving their memory becomes (as often happens today) a commercial success as well, it is because the search for memory grows increasingly. Above all, there is greater demand for those useless things that make life happier and more interesting, that follow the passing of the seasons without anxiety, that make one feel at one with the world. Beware, this is not a whim of the rich, the umpteenth caprice to add to a table already overloaded with food. This is the retrieval of differences, of respect for the variety of things, of an ethical (yes, ethical) value that in the end does not exclude self-interest and pleasure.

Given the success of initiatives concerning "forgotten fruits," we should henceforth call them "rediscovered fruits."

The struggle against time

The fear of hunger has always naggingly affected the history of eating. This fear has at times turned into reality and has brought death. Attempts have been made to cohabit with hunger by organizing a defense against the hardships waiting in ambush. The first of these was to fight time, to invent a personal one, more trustworthy and more secure than the changing and often unpredictable rhythm of the seasons that incessantly assails us.

Of course, humans have adjusted to the rhythm of the seasons and have tried to reap the greatest possible profit. When they imagined a perfect world, they thought of one in which there were no seasons and in which weather was not given to change. Paradise on earth, or the Land of Cockaigne, is a place without seasons in which eternal spring flourishes, food is always available, and its quality is always consistent

To stop time was not only utopian but also the concrete objective of this culture of hunger, which devised efficacious methods for preserving foods to be used outside the "natural" cycle of their growing season. Over the span of centuries, peasant food was based precisely on products that could be kept for long periods, such as grains and legumes that were stored in dry places, open to air or below ground, and could last for many months or even years. Meat, fish and vegetables, which spoil quickly, were subjected to treatments intended to keep them edible longer. This was the primary guarantee of subsistence in a rural economy that could not rely on a daily market or on the capriciousness of the seasons. To preserve food, human ingenuity gave its best: salting, drying, smoking, fermenting—all techniques inspired by the fear of hunger. To the same end, foods were modified by immersing them in vinegar or oil, cooking them in honey or sugar, ingredients that can transform fresh vegetable and animal products into different but preservable products. Cheese and marmalade evolved in this way, as did cold cuts and fish in a barrel.

These techniques later allowed the processing of high-quality foods destined for the marketplace, which also requires preservable foods, given their shipment from one place to another. So many "local specialties," which today constitute the gastronomic patrimony (cheeses and cold cuts in first place) result from skills and techniques that were first developed to conquer hunger. Here is a link, perhaps unsuspected, between the world of hunger and that of pleasure. The cuisine of poverty may have been the laboratory for the creations of haute cuisine.

Diversity as a resource

There is much talk of biodiversity in ecology and culture: how to preserve the wealth of plant and animal life on Earth, how to safeguard the variety of cultures that have respected that wealth. The diversity of species is not only a "natural" reality to be protected, but an outgrowth of human action, an instrument of defense for daily survival.

The primary concern of agricultural societies has always been how to stave off hunger. At times it was a question of real famine caused by poor harvests. More often it was the fear of hunger that could appear at any moment—a perpetual threat against which protection was necessary. The defense strategies were principally two. The first, to figure out methods for keeping foods beyond their natural life cycle. The second, to study biodiversity, to diversify the species so that they might last throughout the year; to select plants of various types so that their presence in the fields and on the table could be extended.

During the Middle Ages, peasants cultivated many different grains (wheat, rye, barley, oats, millet, spelt) precisely to extend the seasons of growth and harvest, and thus obviate the adversities of weather. This prudence was repeated in market gardens where innumerable herbs, root vegetables, and legumes were cultivated. Animals were also raised in large numbers and of various species.

Throughout the centuries, this biodiversity has been one of the primary systems of self-defense of agricultural societies. It came dangerously close to extinction when the concerns of power and profit took precedence over those of local communities. For example, between the eighteenth and nineteenth centuries, many

Italian farmers in the northeast were forced to cultivate corn for their own use because the entire wheat harvest was being shipped to urban markets; in Ireland, at the same time, farmers were eating nothing but potatoes, while choicer products were flowing into the markets of neighboring England. On a global scale, this was one of the greatest disasters caused by the political and economic colonialism of the European powers in the nineteenth and twentieth centuries, which impoverished their subject countries by obliging them to concentrate agricultural production on a few products intended for the international market. The monoculture of coffee, cacao, bananas, sugar cane replaced the variety of local cultures and exposed the farmers to hunger far more dramatic than had ever been experienced in the past.

The lesson of biodiversity is a lesson for all humanity.

Bread of earth

The chronicler Raoul Glaber relates that during the years 1032–1033, during a terrible famine, "an experiment was attempted that has never been seen before." Many people were digging up a kind of white sand, similar to clay, and mixing it with whatever flour and bran was available to produce loaves, in the hope of surviving their hunger."

Faced with accounts of this kind, our most immediate sentiment is one of commiseration: how much effort, how much suffering have humans endured to survive. Such suffering was not confined to the Middle Ages. Similar accounts can be found in texts from the Modern Era, and many articles in today's newspapers are no less dramatic. It is also possible to see this differently: to make bread with earth was nevertheless a controlled response, "rational" in reaction to imminent starvation, before slipping into other types of behavior induced by panic or madness. "To eat plants the way animals do," without preparing or cooking them, was seen as a turning point that signaled the abdication of identity and culture.

They were not debased by recourse to makeshift products, but by renouncing customary practices of preparing and cooking food. To make bread out of earth was still a cultural gesture that utilized techniques of survival devised and transmitted orally by generations of hungry people.

In times of crisis it was *form* that guaranteed the continuity of the alimentary system. In 843, according to the annals of Saint Bertin, "People in many places were reduced to eating earth mixed with a bit of flour and made into the form of bread." Notice the expression of the chronicler: Earth was turned "into the form of bread" (*in panis speciem*). An illusory continuity, this would imply, but life is also made of illusions, images, feelings. Form leads to substance.

Substitute breads are the rule in the history of hunger. Only in extreme cases did people resort to earth. This is not a rhetorical exaggeration: In many parts of the world there are types of clay that really are edible. Used more commonly were inferior grains, higher in yield and more resistant than wheat. Rye, today cultivated primarily in colder regions, either in latitude or altitude, was the first among grains to be used in bread-making. Then there was spelt and farro, barley and millet. There was sorghum, used today solely for forage or to make brooms, but long used as food for humans. Along with grains, vegetables were made into bread, particularly broad beans. In regions of the Apennines flour for bread was made of chestnuts, called "tree bread" in the peasant tradition. In times of great penury acorns were used. This is what the peasants of southern Italy used for bread during the famine of 1058, as the chronicler Goffredo Malaterra informs us.

It was only at this point that wild plants intervened, but they were not necessarily eaten "the way animals do," without preparing them or reducing them to a customary form. "During that year," wrote Gregory of Tours, referring to events that had occurred at the end of the sixth century, "a terrible famine befell Gaul. Many made bread out of grape seeds or with hazelnut flowers; others with the roots of ferns pressed, dried and reduced to powder, mixed with a bit of flour. Others did the same thing with plants cut in the fields." Finally nothing remained but earth, and the metaphor of "Mother Earth" took on a new meaning, no longer abstract but material, organic.

All this was the mark of hunger, real, deep hunger. No less deep was the culture out of which these practices grew: skills consolidated out of experience, the lessons of generations driven by need; an impoverished culture but highly refined. "As is habitual among the poor, they mixed plants with a bit of flour," we read in a German chronicle of the twelfth century.

Scientists and intellectuals as well were concerned with these substitutive practices, teaching the poor what the poor already knew only too well: how to use every available resource in the event of need; how to use, in such cases, products never tasted before. In the recommendations of these authors one recognizes a fundamental principle: the operations of adaptation are all the more intricate the farther one moves away from the norm. For example, in the making of bread, greater attention, greater prudence is required as one goes from wheat to inferior grains, legumes, forage, greens and domestic fruits, and finally wild herbs and roots, pits, and medicinal plants.

In these complicated operations, taste plays a primary role. Ibn al Awwam, an Arab agronomist in Spain, taught how to use fruits that normally would not be edible: Their nature had to be modified, guided by a careful evaluation of their taste. "It is necessary to determine the basic taste of these plants," he wrote, "and try to eliminate it by using suitable procedures; when the taste is gone, the fruit is dried, ground, and then one can begin making bread."

Taste is thus regarded as an infallible guide in the choice and treatment of natural products. Even the world of hunger requires taste to survive.

The right to pleasure

I read in *La Repubblica* (August 28, 2008) that the government of North Korea, or rather the dictator Kim Jong-il, was examining an unusual method for combating the hunger that afflicts many inhabitants of his country. The idea is not to eat more and better, but to eat less and worse. Kim Jong-il ordered his scientists to perfect a new formula for making noodles. By adding soy flour and other ingredients to the traditional ones, these noodles could attenuate and diminish hunger "to a considerable degree," leading people to eat less. In essence, this would be dough that bloats the stomach, reducing the stimulus of appetite.

This is not the first time that the problem of hunger has been approached this way. The eighteenth-century agronomist Giovanni Battara postulated that bread could be made with potato flour and presented this new food in terms not unlike those regarding the extraordinary "invention" of the North Korean government: a bread "somewhat hard to digest" and for that very reason suited to peasants who would feel more sated.

The tone of this account might seem ironic, but the idea that the hunger of peasants can be dealt with through bouts of indigestion, with heavy, rough foods that diminish the desire to eat, is one that recurs often in literature from the Middle Ages all the way to the present. As though by coincidence, it is always the landowners who speak in these terms, and even when the peasants seem to be speaking (as in Battarra's text), it is the landowner who puts his own words into their mouths. That eating may also be a pleasure and that this pleasure is a universal right is an idea that for centuries remained outside the thinking of members of the ruling class, which chose to imagine pleasure as their exclusive privilege. To include "the right to pleasure" among the alimentary objectives of future generations (as appears in the founding manifesto of Slow Food, written by Folco Portinari in 1989) is an act that might look innocuous but is revolutionary.

Rivers of milk and giant tomatoes

In the film *Nuovomondo* (2006), Emanuele Crialese showed America as imagined by some Sicilian peasants preparing to emigrate in the hope of escaping their misery and hunger. For them, America is the land of plenty, where one swims in lakes of milk, where tomatoes and carrots are gigantic.

These grandiose and surreal images are not a gratuitous invention. Ever since the Middle Ages they recur in descriptions of the Land of Cockaigne, the locus of utopia where rivers transport wine (half white, half red); where the walls of houses are made of bass, salmon, and herring, the roofs of prosciutto, and the gutters of sausages; the wheat fields are fenced with pork shoulders and slices of roast meat, and on the street, fat geese are turning on a spit, accompanied by delicious garlic sauces. Descriptions of this kind appear in literary texts of the major European countries with varying characteristics according to the culinary culture and tastes. In Italy, the Land of Bengodi,[1] as described in a novella by Boccaccio, has at its center a mountain of grated parmesan, and on its summit a cauldron brimming with capon broth in which an endless supply of macaroni and ravioli continue to cook. In later centuries this magnificent land will be shown in drawings and prints, always with a mountain in the center, and all around, lakes of butter and milk, while roast pigeons rain down from the sky ready to be devoured.

When Europeans discovered the existence of an unknown continent on the other side of the Atlantic, they imagined it on the model of the Land of Cockaigne. In some way it incarnated Utopia, and they localized it in a specific place, albeit remote and mysterious. In the first half of the sixteenth century, an anonymous poet from Modena hailed it as "The Land of Happy Life," without imagining it could provide new and exotic foods, but rather, in great abundance, the ones he knew and wanted. There "a mountain of grated cheese is all one sees from the plain, and on its peak a cauldron that was brought there," exactly as in Boccaccio's Bengodi. That cauldron, a mile wide, "is always boiling, cooking macaroni," and "no sooner cooked than they are doled out" so that the ones

---

[1] From *godere*, to enjoy.

below are covered with cheese. The fountains pour wine, and rivers of milk make tasty ricotta; partridges and capons are everywhere, and when it rains, "it rains ravioli."

This New World remained in the popular imagination for centuries. Italian peasants who set off for America in the nineteenth century still thought of it as the place where milk flowed in rivers and tomatoes and carrots were enormous. Hunger inspires gastronomic dreams.

FIVE

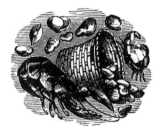

Flavors

Flavor and knowledge

The five senses are like bridges (medieval texts called them "windows") across which humans connect with the world. In various ways these sensory stimuli transmit external reality to us, permitting us to understand it and causing us to act as a consequence. Along with sensations, they provoke intense activity of mental processes. For this reason our language often refers to the senses in a figurative way, attributing to each of them a capacity not only physical but intellectual. "To have an eye" means that we know how to distinguish between situations. "To have a nose" means that we know how to intuit what is going on. "To have a feel" means that we know how to face events with poise, in the proper way. "To have an ear" means that we can recognize the harmony of sounds (this is perhaps the only case in which the comparisons stay within the specific dimension of the sense). "To have taste" means that we know the difference between good and bad, beautiful and ugly. We are "persons of taste" if we can recognize the quality of what we are experiencing, whether a dish, a painting, a novel, or a landscape.

Why has this ability to recognize the nature of things become associated precisely with taste, physiologically intended to perceive flavors? Why, during the Italian and European Renaissance, when the expression "good taste" in the figurative sense first came into use, was reference made specifically to this sense and not to one of the other five senses? The choice was not a given, for in other periods (e.g., in ancient Rome) that kind of ability was represented instead by referring to the nose, the olfactory.

The reason for that choice is that during the Middle Ages scientists and philosophers had assigned to taste a capacity of knowledge superior to the other senses. A Latin text of the thirteenth century entitled *Summa de saporibus*, a treatise on flavors, explained that one can approach reality through vision, hearing, touch, and smell, but "taste alone among the senses is properly suited to seek out the nature of things with perfection," because it is the only one that enters into it, merges completely with it, recognizes flavors deriving directly from that nature, and therefore reveals it. In this way, taste was understood as an essential condition for knowledge, and the analogy between the two words *sapere* and *sapore*[1] did not look like an accidental resemblance, but rather the expression of a substantial affinity between the two concepts.

This is why "taste" or "good taste," in a figurative sense, could become synonymous with experience, knowledge, critical ability.

How many flavors are there?

There are four flavors and each is activated by appropriate receptors located in particular zones of the tongue: sweet at the front, bitter at the back, salty and sour on the right and the left. Many tasting courses hold this to be an indisputable truth.

All "truths" are a product of history, a cultural construct. Aristotle, the major philosopher and scientist of ancient Greece, recognized eight flavors: sweet, fat, bitter, salty, pungent, acid, sour, astringent (later, incorporating fat into sweet, he reduced the

---

[1] The verb to *know* and the noun *flavor*.

number to seven). Medieval texts accepted a variable number from eight to ten, reworking the Aristotelian "canon" and at one point adding the flavor of no-flavor, or insipid. Classifications of this kind lasted into the eighteenth century. Linnaeus, in 1751, distinguished ten flavors: wet, dry, acid, bitter, fat, stringent, sweet, sharp, slimy, salty. Not until 1864 did the anatomist Adolf Fick propose the reduction of flavors to the four categories still recognized today: sweet, salty, sour, bitter. This reversal has its origin in the intuition of a French scientist, Michel Chevreul, who, forty years earlier, established a clear distinction between the sensations of taste, touch, and smell. As of then the concept of flavors narrowed. Whereas the ancient and medieval traditions understood this in a broader sense, even including sensations of a tactile nature such as spicy, astringent and fat, eighteenth-century science tended to identify flavor exclusively as a perception related to taste, to the stimulation of certain receptors rather than others.

The dogma of four flavors seems destined to die as it was born. In the meantime, a fifth flavor, typical of Asian taste, has been officially recognized. Isolated in 1908 by the Japanese chemist Kikunae Ikeda, *umami* is similar to monosodium glutamate; it tastes like meat and cannot be associated with any of the traditionally designated flavors. Moreover, scientists today are trying to revive ideas that for millennia were integral to Western culture before being abandoned during the nineteenth century. The notion of "flavor" is being reconsidered as a complex whole of interactive sensations. If in theory and analysis they function in another manner, being induced by separate senses (taste is taste, touch is touch, smell is smell), in the concrete experience of the individual, sensations mingle and are thus perceived as interconnected—as, in essence, they were regarded by Aristotle and medieval scholars. There is now a movement to include among the flavors cold (the physical-chemical sensation aroused by menthol), and hot (the physical-chemical sensation aroused by hot peppers), a sensation of tingling or electrical stinging. Even fat and astringent, of Aristotelian memory, are in the process of making a grand reentrance.

The nineteenth-century "truth" of four flavors by now is definitely passé.

A longing for sweet

Humans have always thought that sweet is the best flavor. Doctors and scientists had no doubts about considering it the most perfect, the most "suited." A text of the medieval Salerno medical school defined it as "suited to every temperament, age, season, location." By way of confirmation, it was noted that sweet is universally enjoyed. Sweetness was held to be an infallible guide, a sensor capable of revealing the "nature" of any food (today we would say its nutritional properties) and the body's ability to accept it. The instinctive attraction to sweet, manifested from infancy in the sucking of mother's milk, was thus in itself a demonstration that sweet is wholesome.

From the material to the immaterial the distance is short. An inexhaustible quantity of images and metaphors, present in every aspect of our life, uses sweet, both as a noun and as an adjective, to express notions of beauty, pleasantness, serenity. Sweet is rest, sweet is awaking, sweet is the anticipation of a happy event, sweet is a smile, sweet is a caress. Life is sweet, when things go well. The multitude of meanings contained within this word is so vast as to make impossible the selection of an antonym. What is the opposite of sweet? Bitter? Salty? What else? The difficulty of finding an answer comes from the fact that sweet is many things, all of them different, with many contrasts and a single common denominator: the pleasure of the experience.

Every metaphor is built on a concrete reality. Every symbol arises from a primary experience. If in daily language it has been possible to define every pleasurable experience as "sweet," this would mean that it is the flavor of sweet that gives us pleasure. Only the sweetness of sweet makes possible the sweetness of the rest.

However, sweet was not that easy to obtain. Only contemporary society, literally invaded by sugar, has succeeded in the difficult enterprise of creating around it previously unknown images of fear and diffidence that would not have been understood by our ancestors. Over the long arc of our history, the desire for sweet was satisfied exclusively by the work of bees. Then sugar arrived on the scene, introduced to Europe by the Arabs during the Middle Ages and exported by the Europeans to America after the voyages of Christopher Columbus. It was a triumph. The cuisine of the late Middle Ages, the Renaissance, the Baroque is flooded with sugar, used in every dish, every preparation, every course. "There is no food that rejects sugar," wrote Platina in the fifteenth century. In those centuries sweetness was not confined to a particular sector of the menu, as it is today; it was in every part of the menu. The meal might begin with sweetmeats and sweet wine, continue with meat or fish in sweet-salty preparations accompanied by sweet and sour sauces, and end with sweet and spicy confections. Even pasta was generally sauced with sugar and "sweet spices." In the sixteenth century, the botanist Constanzo Felici mentioned the conviction, by then proverbial, that "sugar never spoils the dish." The idea then, both gastronomic and dietary, was that sweet "adjusts" every other flavor.

If sugar became the star performer in the meals of aristocrats, honey continued to be used by the lower classes for a long time, which did not mean that the cuisine of the poor was lacking in sweetness. Countless specialties mark the culinary calendar of peasant society, from private occasions and public festivities to religious and civil holidays. Each significant moment of the year has its particular sweet, and the traditional ones—following a model shared with the cuisine of the elite—place sweet side by side with salty, spicy (the Christmas pepper bread), even bitter and sour. The pleasure of food completes the need to eat. The millet porridge of the fable, which vanquishes hunger thanks to a magic pot, is not only copious but just happens to be sweet: a deep-seated longing, and an ancient one.

Sweet and/or salty

The cart laden with drinks and snacks goes down the aisle of the plane. The first question of the flight attendant is: "Sweet or salty?" One passenger chooses coffee and cookies, another a drink with peanuts.

Perfectly normal. However, the traveling historian cannot help thinking that a mere half millennium ago (not that much if you think about it, a mere fifteen generations) a question like that would have sounded strange.

Everybody has always been able to distinguish between sweet and salty: the taste buds taught us that. In the culture of the Middle Ages and the Renaissance, the contrast between sweet and salty tended to be effaced rather than emphasized. Instead of separating the flavors, there was a preference to mix them. Sweet (which the poor obtained with honey and the rich with sugar) went into everything. The taste for sweet-salty, found in many cuisines throughout the world, was then commonplace even in Europe.

The rule determining this choice was the idea, both dietary and medical, that mixing flavors was beneficial, since each flavor manifests the qualities of a food, and a diet is all the more balanced when it succeeds in bringing together diverse qualities, integrating and tempering the various benefits that each food is capable of providing.

This was the rule that led to alimentary tastes different from those that held sway later on, particularly at the beginning of the seventeenth century. In those days, dietary science went in another direction (focused on the chemistry of foods rather than on their culinary use), and the art of cooking began to favor the separation of flavors. The point was to distinguish one from the other, to maintain each in its position, whether in the preparation of recipes or in the order of the service. It was then that the dessert, final moment of a meal, began to claim exclusive right to the flavor of sweet, eliminating it from meat, fish, pasta, and vegetables, which acquired more decisive characteristics of saltiness.

It is this "revolution in taste"—as Jean-Louis Flandrin termed it—that led to our gustatory custom, which is precisely what made not only possible but normal the question of whether we want something sweet or salty, unless this concerns a food that by definition is outside the realm of a meal. I have in mind the publicity for a "sweet-salty snack," which by calling itself a snack is outside the meal, thus justifying its twin and ambiguous identity of sweet and salty.

No such ambiguity existed in the past. A traveler in the fifteenth century, if he had happened to board a plane, would never have been asked, "Sweet or salty?" because he would not have understood the question, or in any case would have answered, "Sweet *and* salty, of course."

Bitter to the taste

Bitter as bile. Bitter as poison. The revulsion is almost a warning. When the taste buds meet bitterness, the brain decodes it as something not to be eaten, or something that may be harmful. Consequently, it would be dangerous indeed to eliminate the perception of bitterness in food, as was recently proposed by some American researchers.

The history of taste would nonetheless be the poorer without the bitter. The artichoke, cardoon, radicchio, and chicory add flavor to our table, and, in a virtual graph of comparisons among national tastes, Italy would hold first place in appreciation of the bitter. From the Middle Ages on, many observers remarked that Italians like bitter-tasting things. Because Italians are also very fond of sweets (noted centuries ago), it is hardly surprising that Italy has a long tradition of herbal liqueurs, typically bittersweet.

Every city has its own recipe jealously guarded by local tradition. In one place myrtle dominates, in another wild prune, or sorb, or green walnuts, along with sour cherry, gentian, absinthe, rhubarb, quinine . . . a host of plants related by their bitter taste. Even preparations with a citrus base, like limoncello, have a typically bitter flavor.

Even *amaretti* have a taste of bitter almonds, as does coffee, which connoisseurs drink rigorously bitter and which does not lose its bitter aroma even when sugared—the burnt taste that Italian coffee roasters like to give it. Cacao too, which we generally know in its sweetened version, figures in certain traditional recipes as a naturally bitter ingredient.

Bitter is not an easy flavor, but we would be doing nature an injustice if we thought of it only in negative terms, as the opposite of good. Sweet and bitter are not good and evil. Even sweet—the best loved of flavors—in certain cases can become revolting, as the proverb tells us: "Too much sugar spoils the sauce." As for bitter, it is true that in proverbs it is often a metaphor of the sadness of life, but it is also true that it enjoys great respect: "*Cose amare, tienile care,*" bitter things, hold them dearly. The meaning is moral, it tells us that hardships make us grow, just as bitter medicine makes us well. This image of bitter, which makes us appreciate sweet all the more, reveals the idea that both are necessary in life.

When sour was fashionable

A book on the food habits of foreigners who immigrated into the Veneto (edited by Reza Rashidy and published by Coop Consumatori, *Mi racconto . . . ti racconto*) analyzes through a series of interviews what happens when diverse cultures meet and clash, placing traditional values at risk, beginning with those related to food. In some cases the impulse to integrate, to absorb new customs, takes the upper hand; in others, the preservation of traditional ones prevails. More often, the one and the other mix. Food helps people enter into an unfamiliar society that has welcomed them, but also helps them hold on to their own cultural heritage.

Among the stories in the book, one was particularly striking. The Rumanian, Daniel, after having declared (like so many others) that he found Italian food excellent, nonetheless was nostalgic for a flavor that remained in his gustatory memory and that he did not find in the food of Italy, that of sour. Consequently, when he made spaghetti alla carbonara, he added sour cream.

Daniel's testimony struck me as very interesting because it demonstrates the diversity of taste in the food of different countries, but also reminds us (if seen in a historic perspective) of the change in food tastes that has taken place in Western Europe over time. For ancient Romans vinegar was the preferred condiment for all salads, which for that very reason were called *acetaria*.[2] Medieval cooking as well was heavily permeated with sour flavors. The majority of sauces (which invariably accompanied meats and fish) tasted very different from the sweet, smooth taste that comes from butter and oil, stars of the "new" sauces that came into fashion in France and Italy in the early seventeenth century. Medieval sauces were fat-free, based on vinegar, citrus fruits, wine, and *agresto*, the juice of sour grapes. Sour ingredients were added to all kinds of food and were readily mixed with sweet and spicy. The fundamental dietary idea of the time, with which culinary practices were rigorously associated, was that all these flavors had to be present in the preparation of food, because every flavor is enhanced by its opposite. Consequently, any dish that contained them all was balanced and harmonious. This is an idea that is still valid today in the dietary and gastronomic culture of India and China.

In Western taste sour was progressively marginalized, acquiring a negative connotation. "Sour" for us is generally synonymous with unpleasant, even in a figurative sense. In ancient and medieval times, on the contrary, it was appreciated in all its complexity,

---

[2] From *acetum*, vinegar.

analyzed and described with great attention. When medieval scientific texts discussed flavors and their classification, sour was not discussed as a single flavor but was "declined" in multiple variations: acidulous, sharp, acrid, tart, astringent. Today we know that chemically these flavors are variations of a single gustatory typology whose degree of acidity varies, so to speak, quantitatively. Precisely for this reason it is significant that certain cultures and not others are interested in distinguishing the different degrees of acidity and giving each one a name. Linguistic diversification expresses particular attention to what is under discussion, somewhat like the Eskimo language in which there is no word for "white," since in a world where everything is white, the notion of white means nothing in itself and has to be qualified in so many ways: shiny, opaque, bright, dark, light. Similarly, in the Middle Ages, the differentiation among sour flavors had a positive connotation with regard to the perception of those sensations; there was a tendency to esteem them in the gastronomic system. Sour was enjoyed, went with every food, was the fashion.

The taste for spices (and hot pepper)

Spiciness, explained the doctors of the Salerno School, is by nature warm: "It thins, bites, heats, inflames, melts the solid parts." As for its dietary virtues, "sharp flavors, more than others, are appetizers,[3] they raise the temperature of the blood, restore the health of those who suffer from the spleen and more generally from cold temperaments."

Within a philosophy that assigned to flavors the function of "spies" into the nature of food, spiciness held a position of singular prestige during the Middle Ages for dietary reasons. Because digestion was interpreted as a cooking process, the heat afforded by spiciness (and in particular by spices) was considered a cure-all

---

[3] Meaning they facilitate the assimilation of food.

for enhancing the process of metabolism. In addition, there were social and economic reasons. Because of their cost, spices were accessible to few and therefore held great importance as a social distinction. There were also more complex ideas related to the exotic origin of these products, which were thought to come from an earthly Paradise (located, in the geographic imagination of the Middle Ages, precisely in the Asian regions that produced those spices). Dream images, symbols of luxury, and healthful to boot, spices made a fortune for spice merchants, primarily Venetian, who sold them to Western markets.

Spiciness remained for a long time an elite flavor, a sign of social privilege. As late as the sixteenth century, Cristoforo Messibugo, the cookbook writer from Ferrara, proposed using spices in direct proportion to rank. Gentlemen of the highest nobility could use them generously; those of middle rank should reduce the amount.

Transoceanic voyages in search of the Indies, inaugurated by Columbus and continued by a host of navigators, had as their objective (some say primary objective) the conquest of direct access to spice markets. Which indeed happened, with the paradoxical result that spices flowed into European markets in such abundance that their price fell, making them accessible to a larger number of consumers. From then on, they lost their distinctive value and were progressively eliminated from upper-class cuisine, which followed other paths to distinguish itself (the search for soft and velvety flavors, the use of butter in sauces and in pastry).

In the meantime, the hot pepper arrived in Europe from America. Once acclimated and cultivated in various regions, it finally made spiciness popular. As of then, spice was no longer a mark of social distinction.

The taste of smoke

Is smoke a substance or an accident? This Aristotelian-sounding question (it was Aristotle who made the distinction between substantive elements in the nature of things and occasional or accidental ones) is central to a curious story, probably of Oriental origin, that appears in *Novellino*, a collection of anecdotes and tales compiled in Florence in the thirteenth century. It is the story of a poor Saracen who, having nothing to eat besides a piece of bread, stood next to the steaming pot of a street vendor holding his piece of bread in the smoke to give it some flavor: "and when the bread was saturated with the smoke that rose out of the food, he bit into it." The cook, who had sold next to nothing that day, demanded that he be paid, maintaining that the smoke, a product of the food he had prepared, was his property. They began quarreling and so the question was brought to the sultan, who summoned the wise men of the court and listened to their opinions. One of them argued that smoke cannot be considered an integral part of food, because it vanishes and provides no nutrition. Others said, on the contrary, that it is part of the substance, as it is generated by it. After listening to all of them, the sultan reached his decision. He gave the poor man a coin and ordered him to drop it on the ground. To the cook he said, "Payment can be assumed, given the sound that came from it."

This amusing fable, which contains an interesting philosophical and scientific disquisition, regards smoke as the carrier of perfumes and aromas. Smoke not only carries odors, but in certain cases even generates them. Specifically, this occurs when smoke is used to preserve meat, fish, and cheese. The primary purpose of this process is to preserve the food, to envelop in smoke a product, perhaps preventively salted, so as to dry it and eliminate the moisture that could cause its rapid deterioration. Throughout the peasant world, and above all (though not only) in cold regions, this ancient technique assured the longer duration of food and provided a defense against the threat of hunger. In the Middle Ages, many rural houses had smoke rooms to treat the winter food supply in this manner. Even a sovereign like Charlemagne ordered the administrators of his properties to "oversee with much care and great cleanliness" the preparation of smoked meats, such as salamis and sausages.

Treatments like these make foods take on a particular taste, which in some cases are expressly desired. Smoke is not only an odor but a flavor, and one can grow accustomed to this flavor, as to any other, and even become fond of it. Drinks have also been smoked One has only to think of certain kinds of whiskey. In such practices it becomes difficult, if not impossible, to separate reasons of necessity from those of taste. This is precisely what is so fascinating about the history of food: the extraordinary ability of humans to transform anxiety over survival into occasions of pleasure.

How chocolate became sweet

Cacahuatl. This is what the ancient Mayas called a Central American plant whose seeds, once roasted, peeled, ground, and reduced to a powder, were boiled with pepper, chili pepper and ginger, and occasionally made milder by the addition of a little honey and a paste of corn flour. The resulting beverage, bitter and spicy, was drunk by the priests during religious ceremonies and offered to the gods, who were said to prefer this to anything else. This is why Linnaeus called it *Theobroma*, meaning precisely "food of the gods."

When Europeans invaded America, this cocoa drink immediately aroused their curiosity but was not to their taste. Their cuisine abounded in sugar, a product then unknown in America, which the Arabs had brought to Europe during the Middle ages and rapidly became a mark of social prestige. The menus of Renaissance courts began with sweetmeats and continued with sweetened dishes: meat drenched in sugar, pasta sprinkled with sugar, sweet-salty tortes, and on and on until the closing desserts. It was therefore no surprise if chocolate was also welcomed in Europe, on condition that it be softened and sweetened. The powerful spices of the American tradition (pepper, chili pepper, ginger) were replaced with the more delicate aromas of vanilla, musk, amber. Above all, it was the massive use of sugar that changed the flavor of the drink whose Mayan name of *chacauhaa* (Aztec, *xocolatl)* was transformed into *chocolate* in Spanish and English, *chocolat*, in French, and *cioccolata* in Italian.

In Europe, as in America earlier, chocolate remained an elite drink for a long time. It was the aristocracy above all that adopted it. Because foods are not only edible substances but also social images, it became almost a symbol of the lifestyle of the nobility in the seventeenth and eighteenth centuries. Bourgeois culture viewed aristocrats as "idle," contrasted with the activity of merchants, the productivity of industrialists, and the acumen of enlightened intellectuals, who preferred to gather in coffee shops. The two products, chocolate and coffee, ended up representing two opposing ways of life. Chocolate met with considerable success among the religious, since it is a drink (albeit highly nutritious) and thus permissible on fast days. In certain countries, such as Spain, it continued to be prepared with water, following American usage. Elsewhere, as in Italy or England, milk was preferred to water. In the eighteenth century chocolate began to be produced in solid form, destined to have a great future.

Experiments of every kind flourished on chocolate. The Florentine court of the Medici became famous in seventeenth-century Europe for a secret recipe that gave chocolate the exciting perfume of jasmine (it was later learned that the secret was in mixing jasmine not into the hot liquid, as others tried to do, but into the cacao powder, which was then dissolved in milk). Chocolate enriched with bits of amber was long held to be a formidable tonic for a listless body. In the eighteenth century there were those who proposed mixing cacao with wine or beer, with coffee or tea, with spirits, and even with broth, to achieve salty flavors instead of sweet.

Experimentation has not ceased. Chocolate is being joined with balsamic vinegar, uniting sweet and sour; with mint, which opposes the taste of freshness to heat, diverting the sensation of sweetness; with hot and fragrant spices, which seem to take us back to where this story began, in the jungles of central America where Mayan and Aztec priests drank cacao mixed with chili peppers and ginger while celebrating their rites. Not to mention cacao used as a condiment in meat dishes, already in practice in the haute cuisine of the Renaissance and still used in traditional dishes such as the Tuscan *"dolceforte,"*[4] and similar preparations. If someone tells us today that chocolate is good even when salty, we are hardly surprised. We would do history a disservice if we considered that person an innovator.

The taste of canned foods

We are accustomed to thinking of canned food as the very definition of "not fresh": on the one side, vegetables freshly picked and immediately brought to the table, on the other, a metal container that replaces freshness with shelf life.

This was not the intention of the first food industries, which, in the nineteenth century, offered consumers peas and asparagus in cans. The publicity surrounding these new products insisted on the very opposite idea: at last, preserved food that can reach your table *fresh*.

Why? For the simple reason that traditional processes for preserving food, handed down either in the modes used in homes or in the preparation of products for markets, were all based on the addition of substances—salt, oil, vinegar, sugar—which in various ways modified, and in some cases altered the "natural" flavor of foods. Vegetables kept in salt (such as sauerkraut) are no longer what they once were. Vegetables in oil, or vinegar, undergo a similar modification of their natural taste. Fruits in syrup or as jams, obtained from cooking with the addition of sugar, are distinctly new products. All of these are delicacies, of course—today's market for regional specialties continues to be an outgrowth of those

---

[4] Used in braised beef and rabbit, it imparts a dense flavor rarely recognized as coming from chocolate.

millennial practices—and rightly so, since delicacies differ from their original substance.

The use of the can, in which fruits and vegetables were enclosed and then subjected to boiling (Nicolas Appert, who invented this technique in the early nineteenth century, explained that this procedure also made the container antiseptic and sterilized the product), allowed for the first time the preservation, within certain limitations, of the original appearance and flavor of the product. This is, paradoxically, why canned food could become synonymous with fresh food, and was so publicized by its producers: Appert in France, Durand in England, Hahn in Germany, Cirio in Italy.

The food industry has also devised other ways of preserving food without altering it. Artificial cold, produced by refrigerators (later by freezers), which appeared for the first time in the mid-nineteenth century, was and remains the ideal process. Here too is the paradox of a process of preservation that gives what is not fresh the characteristics of freshness. More recently, the techniques of vacuum packing have been developed. By eliminating the air in the container, this process preserves the contents. Preservation in a "modified environment" that affects the gasses present in the wrapping is the latest conquest of alimentary technology.

These are not fresh vegetables, to be sure, but we can nonetheless be satisfied with the resemblance, and during the growing season let us occasionally pop into the garden to taste "genuine" flavors.

SIX

Pleasure and Health

"What tastes good is good for you"

The relationship between pleasure and health is often perceived today as adversarial. Nevertheless, in our traditional culture it has been experienced as an alliance providing reciprocal advantage. The idea that pleasure might be healthful, that "what tastes good is good for you" (as prescribed by a Milanese doctor of the fourteenth century, Maino de'Maineri), is fundamental to ancient dietetics. It arose from the conviction that signals from the body, which prompt us to desire one food rather than another, help us recognize, through the pleasantness of their taste, which foods the body requires. Within this tradition, the "rules of health" developed by the medical establishment were primarily alimentary rules, understood not in a restrictive sense (a distorted notion of diet, which for the ancients meant "a style for daily living"), but as directions for establishing gastronomic practices.

Ancient dietetics, which remained in place until the end of the seventeenth century, was based on Aristotle's physics and classified foods according to four conditions held to be produced by the combination of the four natural elements—earth, fire, water, air—which were paired two by two: cold and hot, wet and dry.

In cooking, the object was to eliminate excesses, to prepare and combine ingredients in a way that would balance their qualities. To achieve this, the cook had to work on two major fronts: cooking techniques and modes of pairing. For example, if a product was classified as "wet," it was best to cook it without water, which meant roasting; a "dry" product was best tempered by water, or boiling. The same rule applied to the foods served on the side. Meat of a "hot" nature should be accompanied by a sauce or a food of the opposite nature.

In this game of combinations, what counted was not only theoretical rules but also the experience, practice, and sensitivity of individuals. The success of these pairings and solutions found immediate approval in that they were pleasing to the taste (this explains the custom of combing certain fruits, such as melon, judged very cold and very wet, with foods that are very hot and very dry, such as prosciutto and salami). The proximity of dietetics and gastronomy was reinforced by language that covered both. The concepts of hot, cold, wet, dry were reflected in the perception of their physical characteristics. That water was cold and broth hot was not only a medical classification but a sensory observation. There was consequently a continuous exchange between daily experience and conceptual elaboration, culinary practices and theoretic reflections on the nutritional value of foods.

Today dietetic science has greatly changed; it no longer speaks the language of physics but of chemistry and has thus moved away from sensory evidence. It nonetheless continues to affect profoundly the way we sit down to a meal. There is, for example, a very clear, even if not immediate, relationship between the discovery of vitamins, dating from the beginning of the twentieth century, and "the fashion" of not overcooking foods, typical of our time (whereas until the previous century the rule was that everything had to be well cooked). The dialectic between gastronomy and dietetics, between pleasure and health, seems to be a permanent factor of history.

The law of opposites, between kitchen and pharmacy

At first glance kitchen and pharmacy would seem to be worlds apart. There is a word in Italian that relates the two, a word we often use both in the kitchen and in the pharmacy: *ricetta,* recipe.[1] If the word is the same, there must be some common ground. That common ground is the idea that nature, often hostile, can compensate through artificial preparations produced by human inventiveness. *Ricetta* comes from the Latin *recipe*, which means "take," choose. Take things from nature, selecting them with care, and combine them in such a way as to make them useful.

Useful to health, that is. This is taken for granted in the case of a drug, whose purpose is to fight illness, a physiological failure; a drug is supposed to restore an equilibrium that was lost. The fundamental principle, ever since Hippocrates invented Western medicine 2,500 years ago, has always been the law of opposites: to restore good health one must use substances of a character opposite to those that caused the illness. As the Roman doctors said, *contraria contrariis sanantur:* "opposites are healed with opposites."

The same logic presided over kitchen usages. They too, rigorously bound to medical theories, were based on the law of opposites. Since nature was thought to be imperfect, it must be manipulated and corrected, thereby achieving an equilibrium that does not exist in nature but that is necessary for human health. Sauces, central to ancient and medieval cooking, were used to "correct" the nature of foods as well as their accompaniments, in order to obtain a balanced dish. Other pairings served the same purpose. Each food was corrected by a food of an opposite nature.

It is precisely this idea of correction, of human intervention to adjust nature artificially, that brings together the kitchen and the pharmacy. The sauces that the cook serves with meat and fish are

---

[1] In English the word was also formerly used for both meanings; now *prescription* is used in the pharmacy.

like the antidotes prepared by the pharmacist to cure illness. And if the pharmacist knew the secret to a universal antidote for all illnesses—the famous *teriaca,* concocted from a dozen vegetable and animal substances, including snake blood (the animal which, for that very reason, is still today the symbol of pharmaceutical science)—in the kitchen as well, substances were sought to remedy every imperfection, substances that varied according to the rank and capabilities of the consumer. For centuries, spices, regarded as the universal improvement of all foods, were reserved for the upper classes. Peasants had to content themselves with garlic, to which ancient tradition attributed equally universal powers, which explains why it was called "the teriaca of the peasantry."

Watermelon, salt and pepper

For a historian concerned with food, a trip to distant lands can be an occasion to rediscover customs and choices that once marked his own culture.

I happened to be visiting Vietnam when, for the first time, I saw watermelon and other fruits such as pineapple and melon seasoned with a mixture of salt and chili pepper. This pairing, which at first sight can be disconcerting (until later acknowledging it on my own tongue as thoroughly convincing), in the eyes of the historian was an immediate and easy recognition because it evoked the rules of the ancient science of dietetics. Like the Hippocratic doctrine in Greece, which viewed the world as a proper balance of opposites, Asian philosophers, particularly in India and China, produced a system similarly based on the idea of opposing pairs: the Taoist tradition of yin and yang, which is the model for universal harmony, maintained by the coexistence of the two principles of negative and positive.

In the case of food, this signified the promotion of practices intended to modify the nature of each food with its opposite, pairing, for example, wet and cold foods, as many kinds of fruit were classified, with their opposites: salt which dries, spices which heat. The salt-hot pepper pairing is a living expression of this culture, an integrated and "total" response to the dual requirement of compensation. This is not the only approach possible: In other culinary traditions salted products replace salt, such as cold cuts and cheeses. In Italy it is customary to serve prosciutto with melon, cheese with pears. In Turkey, watermelon is still eaten with cheese. In France melon can be served with salt or more commonly with port (intended to oppose the "coldness" of the fruit).

Today in the West the rules of ancient dietary science no longer represent a conscious and explicit cultural reference. Those traces that remain (in gastronomy as well) are like the fossils of a forgotten past. In the East, on the other hand, that science continues to be recognized (in Asiatic countries traditional medicine lives alongside modern medicine). This is why a trip to a distant land can in some ways resemble a voyage into time.

Monthly diets

"In September ripe fruits are salutary, pears in wine, apples with goat milk, a pleasing and diuretic drink. Then, open a vein and eat plants with seeds. In September the trees provide apples and pleasing fruits; you should also eat fresh goat cheese. This will not prevent you from taking medicines."

These are recommendations that we read in a text from the Salerno school, the oldest European medical school, dating from the tenth century. As was habitual in medieval dietary literature, this text indicates the rules to be followed each month of the year for the appropriate expedients to accompany seasonal variations. From Hippocrates on, ancient doctors had already insisted on the need to adapt one's regimen to the changing conditions of the environment. Medieval medicine believed in translating these teachings into simple precepts, practical rules of daily use. Thus was born the *regimina mensium,* monthly regimen—a catalogue of things to do or not do each month.

The purpose of the prescriptions is at times clear, at others less so. Sometimes they are directly related to the rhythms of nature; other times they are more theoretical and bookish. In the short notice regarding the month of September, quoted here merely as an example, to "open a vein" refers to the established practice of bloodletting, which traditional medicine recommended for cleansing the body and liberating it of excessive "humors." During the heat of summer this practice was suspended, as was that of purges and other medicines for regulating the body's equilibrium. In September, with the return of a temperate climate, one could begin anew.

The insistence on goat's milk, either as a drink or as a condiment in the preparation of apples, is a medical rather than an alimentary prescription. Milk was rarely drunk in the Middle Ages, because it did not keep well. Normally, it was turned into cheese, fresh or aged, even if doctors (as in this case) recommended drinking fresh milk when possible. Fruit, abundant in that season, was to be eaten very ripe. This advice, still valid today, was insistent to the point of being obsessive during the Middle Ages, out of fear of the acidity of sour fruit, and its "cold" and "wet" nature, which was believed to jeopardize the health of the organism. To prevent this risk, it was often advised to cook it in wine, as stated in this quotation. "Plants with seeds," mentioned in the text, are probably vegetables to be eaten copiously in September.

Food and medicine, as always, come together in these prescriptions. The underlying philosophy is the adjustment of one's lifestyle (*diet* understood in its broad and total sense) to the changing of climatic conditions, with a continual effort of adaptation, difficult and at times stressful. It was not without cause that the ancient Greeks thought men were healthy and robust where the climate is stable and without seasons. This is what Herodotus wrote about the Egyptians and the marvelous region in which they lived.

The language of the navel

It is fashionable to wear short tee-shirts that reveal the navel; it shows how agile the body is and how lean and tight the belly is. Strangely enough, a few centuries ago the same thing communicated the very opposite. I am thinking of certain Etruscan sarcophagi that show the deceased with his robe slightly raised above the navel to reveal a well-rounded belly, not to excess though certainly not flat; in fact, decidedly prominent. The image of the deceased that is left for posterity to meditate is that he lived happily, he ate, he nourished his body with care.

Not only among the Etruscans but in all traditional societies, unlike today, fat was not an enemy to be avoided, but rather a respected and appreciated friend. The difference between the two perspectives, very simply, is the difference between hunger and plenty. In a world dominated by hunger (or even just the fear of hunger), the desire for food was always left unsatisfied and the possibility of eating copiously and regularly was reserved for the few. This is why "fat" never had a negative connotation. In the societies that preceded ours, it was, rather, a positive one. "A fat people" was what the rich Florentine middle class was called in the late Middle Ages, in recognition of its economic and political successes. "Fat" was the definition of the city of Bologna, "*Bologna la grassa*," to express its affluence, its well-stocked market, the ease of life for the many strangers (students and professors) who flocked from every corner to attend the university. Matteo Bandello, celebrating the sumptuousness of Milan, wrote that it "is the most opulent and best supplied city in Italy where more than anywhere else one expects the table to be rich [*grassa*] and well laden."

This culture went through our history, projecting on fat—the fat both of food and of body—all kinds of positive images. From the fatted calf of the Bible (the best, the one chosen for grand occasions), to the edict of Diocletian, who, in the third century, when setting maximum prices for food products, made cuts of fat meat the highest, we see a succession of evaluations with economic, esthetic, and symbolic implications. Julius Caesar's witticism, which Shakespeare took from Plutarch, "Beware the lean and hungry man," seems to introduce a moral variant. Men, like food, are all the more trustworthy when they are fat, or at least "meaty."

The esthetic ideal was the consequence of such views. If medieval art presents images of elongated knights and ladies, Renaissance and Baroque art represent the triumph of rotundity, of sturdy nudes, not only feminine, in paintings and sculpture. Even a generation ago, who hadn't heard a grandmother or a mother say: "Oh, you're so nice and fat"? Today this does not happen, and if it did it would be most unappreciated. The society of plenty has canceled old fears and created new ones, replacing the fear of penury with the fear of excess, the fear of thinness with the fear of obesity. Doctors and dietitians invite us to a daily confrontation with the scale, not without reason, now that diseases of excess, once reserved for elite societies, have become a mass phenomenon democratically accessible to all. Mental attitudes and esthetic values have changed along with economic structures and lifestyles. We still expose our navel, but for other reasons.

Fat, meaning meat

The "festival of the fat bull," which is celebrated annually in Carrù, in Piedmont, is heavy with historical significance. It goes back to an ancient culture, apparently dead (but it may only be dormant), that attributed to fat values far removed from those of today, making it symbolic of prosperity, security, wealth—a culture, moreover, that identified meat as the ideal fat food.

Other foods can also be fat. "White and fat" was the exquisite cheese that a French bishop presented to Charlemagne in the hope of obtaining his good will. Even fish can be fat. However, fat is primarily and principally to be found in meat, and it is from this equivalence that the traditional opposition of the two alimentary models arose, the "fat" diet and the "lean" diet, rigorously alternated in the liturgical calendar and characterized, respectively, by the presence or absence of meat. To eat "lean" means the food of Lent, the eves of holidays, the days during the week dedicated to abstinence, when "lean" equals meatless. On the other hand, to eat "fat" means a meat diet. In medieval culinary texts, and even into the Modern Era, the distribution of foods and the distinction between recipes often follow this basic dichotomy.

The meaning of abstinence lies in restraining the primal alimentary desire: meat, fat. Desire, *desiderio*, had the dual Latin meaning of yearning and lacking. Meat was often missing from the tables of the populace, but not the yearning for it. As for fat, "If I were king I would drink only fat," muses a peasant in a seventeenth-century French text. Lords and landowners always had it in abundance. Gout and circulatory diseases caused by too much food, meat in particular, were almost a sign of class privilege in certain periods of history.

"Give me a slice of lean meat," a request that we often hear at the butcher's, would have sounded bizarre in another period, an incomprehensible oxymoron. Now that lean meat is desirable, the fat bull of Carrù is another fossil of a lost civilization.

"Indigestion does not bother peasants"

In his treatise *Agrarian Practice* (1778) Giovanni Battara records a dialogue between a peasant and his sons, Mingone and Ceccone. The father is pointing out the usefulness of planting potatoes that will provide relief from their daily hunger, and can even be used to make bread. One has only to mix potatoes with an equal part of wheat flour (this was also recommended by the famous Parmentier).[2] "And what if we made it only with potatoes?" Mingone asks. "It can be done," replies his father, "but bread made that way is said to be all the harder on the digestion." Surprisingly, this does not

---

[2] Antoine-Augustin Parmentier (1737–1813), French pharmacist and chemist.

disturb Mingone one bit; on the contrary, he is delighted by the idea because, he explains, "Indigestion does not bother peasants; it makes them feel more sated."

Is a bad indigestion—to keep at bay as long as possible the desire to eat, too often frustrated and frustrating—the most that an eighteenth-century peasant could hope for? Or a medieval one, or even a later one? Many texts refer to this, attributing to peasants a taste for coarse, heavy foods, useful for bloating the stomach rather than stimulating the pleasure of the palate. There was even a hero, Bertoldo, in Giulio Cesare Croce's literary epic, who, "undernourished" by the delicate, refined foods of the king's table, protests and finally dies "from having been deprived of turnips and beans."

No peasant of the Middle Ages or the sixteenth century or the seventeenth ever had a chance to tell us what he liked to eat in his own voice. Literature expresses the culture of the *others*, the landowners and aristocrats; the image of the peasant that emerges is deformed by perspectives related to easily recognizable class interests. At the very least, we should recognize that the alimentary choices of the peasantry, dictated primarily by need, reflect habits rather than tastes—two notions that Jean-Louis Flandrin has taught us to keep separated. The cleverness of so many literary representations lies in the shift from one notion to another, transforming bitter necessity into conscious dietary preference. This said, it is undeniable that lightness has little place in the culinary traditions of the peasantry, more inclined to strong flavors and solid consistencies.

As it happens, the situation is not very different if one looks at the other side of the social picture. The alimentary habits of medieval aristocracy, long in place among the ruling classes of modern Europe, were also alien to a culture of lightness. In that case it was not for reasons of hunger or the fear of an empty stomach, but rather for strength: the aspiration toward a robust, vigorous body, the indispensable requisite for valor in war and for social supremacy. "He is satisfied with a modest repast and is thus not worthy of reigning over us." With these words of contempt, the aspiration of the duke of Spoleto to become king of the Franks, at the end of the ninth century, was denied.

The lightness of the monk

In contrast to the culture of the aristocracy, taken from the myth of physical power and a healthy appetite, and the culture of the peasantry, marked by pangs of hunger and dreams of a full belly, medieval monastic culture clung to alimentary choices that favored lightness—for centuries a decidedly minority virtue. Detachment from food, sobriety, abstinence, voluntary fasting, this was the best way for the monk to express his detachment from corporal desires, his renunciation of "the world." The lightness of the body, enabling the soul to rise, was a symbolic objective but even more, a material one: to forget that the body exists, that it has physical weight; to prevent it from interfering with mental acrobatics. "He ate as though he were not eating, he drank as though he were not drinking." The behavior of the saints, which pushes the logic of corporal lightness to the extreme, is evoked as a veritable utopia; an impossible oxymoron.

In noble circles as well, at the end of the Middle Ages, dietary precepts appeared regarding the delicacy and lightness of food, along with its nutritive value. Whereas a sovereign like Charlemagne, a few centuries earlier, reveled in coarse game (boar, deer, bear) as a symbol and instrument of power, the alimentary image of the valorous warrior, the new nobility began to follow different eating styles, related more to courtly life than to warring, to the elegance of dress rather than to the strength of the muscles. The intellectual aristocracy of the fourteenth and fifteenth centuries, and later of the Renaissance, which did not surround itself with painters, musicians, and poets by chance, represented its new identity not by eating little—this continued to remain inconceivable—but by shifting attention to meats of another kind, primarily birds and poultry (pheasant, partridge, quail, capon), which dietetic science regarded as less "fattening." Even the monastic diet had always manifested a certain tolerance for the meat of birds, whereas that of quadrupeds had been strictly prohibited. Lightness versus heaviness. Dietary values and ethical choices.

The theme of health also entered at times into monastic reflections on food. On one side, the lightness of the body allows one to forget it; on the other, it guarantees well-being. These would seem to be contradictory views, one *against* the body, the other *for* its protection; diffidence and respect, care and neglect. These very contradictions can be seen today in various aspects of bourgeois culture that, in the end—while protected from the fear of hunger and attentive to an efficient and active body, though not without residual suggestions of a penitential nature—adopted the monastic line over that of the aristocracy and the peasantry.

When pleasure frightens

The difference between slow food and fast food is often understood in terms of time and rhythm: slowness versus speed. This seems to be a misleading interpretation, because the difference is rather in the willingness (or, obversely the indifference) to prepare, offer, and savor food *attentively*. That takes time but not necessarily a lot. What is required is *attention*, to the choice of ingredients, the cooking method, the succession of flavors, manner of presentation, choice of company to share the food. This attention is not opposed to speed but to haste, to distraction, which is equally pertinent to a meal at home or dinner at a restaurant, a drink at a bar or a sandwich at a lunch counter. (Don't tell me that they are all the same; not even school lunches are all the same, nor even meals on airline trays.)

Inattention to food is not only caused by occasional necessity, individual preference, or personal phobia. (I have the painful memory of an English colleague who pulled a cold chicken out of the fridge, proclaiming with pride that food did not interest him.)

There is in our history a veritable *culture of distraction,* of Christian origin, related to diffidence toward the body and the association of pleasure with sin, which leads to the recommendation not to make food a source of pleasure, not to dedicate too much attention to it, to experience *distractedly* this fundamental of our physical existence. Christian tradition is certainly not monolithic on these matters; on the contrary, it is highly inconsistent and in some ways contradictory, but the power of that particular message has long conditioned our relationship to food.

A few stories, taken from late-ancient and medieval hagiographies, will demonstrate what I mean. Among the biographies of hermit saints who sought asceticism in the solitude of the desert, the one about abbot Pior tells us that "he ate while walking." To someone who asked him the reason for this strange behavior, he explained: "I want eating to be a superfluous occupation." To another who made the same inquiry, he said: "While I eat I do not want my soul to experience any material pleasure." In short, Pior trained himself to eat while distracting his own body so as to make it unaware that he was eating; otherwise he would have run the risk of enjoying the experience.

Another hermit, Sisoe, immersed himself so deeply in thought of God that he no longer remembered whether he had eaten or not. If one of his disciples invited him to take food, he would reply, "Haven't we already eaten?" If the answer was "No," Sisoe would then resign himself to eating something, inattentively, of course. Another pious figure, Abbot Pastore, when called to eat, went so unwillingly, so much "against his will," that at times he even wept.

The ideal of these men would have been not to eat at all, to avoid being a slave to the body. Bishop Erardo's practices of abstinence went to intolerable limits in his quest to determine "what the possibilities were of living without food." Since eating is nonetheless necessary, (among medieval Christian writers the image of the body as "a merciless tax collector" frequently appears), the least one can do is to take no pleasure in it. To separate pleasure from necessity was the impossible challenge of many Christian ascetics. Impossible, because food, as Saint Girolamo explained, inevitably activates both sensory mechanisms and the experience of pleasure. Here are the "anti-culinary" practices that were intended to eliminate the olfactory appeal of food. When Abbot Lupicino returned to his monastery and noticed, from the fragrance emanating from the kitchens, that the monks were preparing succulent fish and other tasty dishes, he ordered that everything be ground together and made into a single indistinguishable gruel (*pulmentum*). If I had to find a kitchen implement particularly suited to this kind of gastronomic culture it would surely be the blender.

One also comes across figures who tried to thwart the taste buds by taking nutriments in other ways. Abbot Lupicino, during a long fast, was assailed by an irresistible thirst, but not wishing to experience the pleasure of drinking, contrived to absorb it through the skin by immersing his arm in a pitcher filled with water. In this case the ideal way of ingesting food is the drip method.

Taste, in short, is the great enemy, because it teaches us to distinguish, appreciate, evaluate. Also among the stories of the "desert fathers" is the one about Macario, who speaks of having met the devil in the shape of a man with many bowls of food hanging from his neck. "I am bringing taste to your brothers," explained the demon-man when asked what he was doing. "I am, moreover, bringing many things so that if one food is not pleasing, they can try another, and if that other does not satisfy them, I can offer them yet another, and still another, until they find one to their liking."

Not choose. Not appreciate. Not distinguish. Not pay attention to the food but eat it without noticing. This is the real fast food. Not without reason is the English word *fast*, in the sense of speed, also the word for abstaining from food. Abbot Pior is the true prophet of this fast food, he who ate while wandering through the desert, slowly, unhurriedly, but forcing himself to ignore food, to forget his own body.

Monastic gastronomy

Monks and gastronomy: a winning combination even if paradoxical, because the relationship of the monastic world with food has been characterized in an ambiguous, contradictory manner. Moderate, reasonable choices for a way of life, like those recommended at the start of the Middle Ages by Saint Benedict of Norcia, always conflicted with rigid, often severe attitudes toward physical pleasures, first among them the pleasure of food, as pernicious as necessary, because one has to eat. It is therefore a fundamental pleasure, unavoidable, precursory to other physical attentions, other vices and pleasures. This is how the fathers of monastic thinking saw it at the dawn of medieval Christianity, observing that Adam himself was stained with original sin resulting from his hunger for a forbidden fruit—in essence, a sin of gluttony. The practices of abstinence and fasting, prescribed by every monastic order, are expressions of this culture, hardly favorable when it comes to food.

Herein lies the paradox. It was these very rules of abstinence that led to concerns of a truly gastronomic nature. The exclusion of meat, which represented the basic choice in the monastic diet though varying from community to community, made necessary the patient development of alternative products such as vegetable soups, pasta dishes, eggs and cheese, not to mention fish, which was the closest alternative to meat. In addition, there were jams and preserves of every kind, which could provide the monks with total self-sufficiency to prevent them from "straying" (in the words of Saint Benedict) in search of food outside the community. Monastic solitude, conducive to meditation and prayer, thus produced a crooked parallel to peasant society, similarly concerned with keeping an even alimentary scale to protect itself from the sempiternal threat of famine.

This is how the monastery could become—almost in spite of the kind of life that governed it—a formidable center of gastronomic culture. The iconic gluttonous monk, stereotype of a venerable oral and literary tradition, grew out of these conditions. Added to this was the fascination with "secrecy," the practices and habits jealously guarded from worldly corruption. The attribution of "monastic" could thus become an unequivocally positive value. "How many cheeses," asked the sociologist Léo Moulin, "are not of monastic origin?" As to their origins, I wouldn't know, but when it comes to marketing, such an attribution certainly works—even if it unfairly disregards the shepherds and peasants who worked with and for the monks, thus contributing significantly to their gastronomic heritage and our own.

Which is why the collective imagination associates the monastic tradition not only with penitence and mortification, but also with the history of wholesome, tasty products tenderly produced—flavorful soups, medicinal herbs, tonic elixirs, and delectable cheeses.

Philosophizing gluttony

The attention given to food by medieval monks reached levels of refinement that moralists condemned as excessive and unbecoming. Indirectly, these very polemics reveal the existence of gastronomic attitudes that, mistakenly perhaps, we cannot imagine in such eras and cultures.

Let us take a text of the eleventh century, *On the Perfect Formation of a Monk* by Pier Damiani, one of the most uncompromising believers in the mortification of the body, hermitic asceticism, temperance, and abstinence from food. In view of the fact, he writes, that temperance is the first defense of chastity, which is the fundamental duty and virtue of the monk, it must be with him every day, even when "gluttony itches." This means not eating excessively, not engaging in lavish meals, not indulging in wine. What is to be avoided first of all is listening when gluttony speaks, argues, philosophizes, when it invites us to discourse on the differences of color or aroma of one wine or another.

To exemplify the futility of the arguments suggested by this "philosophizing gluttony" (*gulae philosophantis argumenta*), Pier Damiani recounts an imagined discussion among drinkers that goes more or less like this: "This wine is made slightly tart by a touch of the Leporina grape; that one is enervated by the weakness of the Venacorica; another is reddened by the presence of Porrotasia; this one is gilded by the golden splendor of the Mareotide; this one should not be harvested, it has gone bad and nauseates me; this one has received baptism [too watered]; in this wine there is surely a lot of the Aminea grape, but the Retica seems almost to overwhelm it. . . ." Don't you be concerned, Pier Damiani tells the monk to be instructed, about knowing "how much [the wine] tastes of Argite, how much of Rodia, how much sharpness and how much mellowness is achieved by blending the early purple grapes with the late-harvest Greek ones." These are vulgar concerns, the concerns of "a philosopher of gluttony."

If all this is a prescription for *not* doing something, it signifies that it *was* done, that during the Middle Ages there existed in certain social groups a highly refined ability to distinguish the grapes that went into a wine, to discuss its provenance, and evaluate its quality with connoisseurship.

Let us look at another example, another polemical text against those who, having forgotten their monastic vows, engage in disquisitions over wine instead of the mysteries of creation. In the twelfth century, Saint Bernard of Clairvaux, founder of the Cistercian order and great disciplinarian of monastic life, in a work entitled *Apologia of Abbot William*, attacked the monks at Cluny for inveterately drinking strong spiced wines, ignoring the Benedictine rule, and grossly misinterpreting Saint Paul's recommendation (in the first letter to Timothy) to cure a stomach ache with a little wine. "Evidently," Bernard remarks sarcastically, "ever since we became monks we all have sensitive stomachs." In the lines following, Bernard deplores the excessive attentions given to tasting, sniffing, selecting the finest wine: "I am ashamed to say it, but during a single meal you can see a cup half full sent away three or four times, so that after having inhaled, rather than drunk, various types of wines, and after having licked rather than gulped them, at last, with knowing taste and quick recognition, one wine is chosen, considered by many to be the choicest. . . . Shall we say that this too is caused by the sensitivity of the stomach? In my view this only enables one to drink more and with greater pleasure."

If "gastronomy" means eating and drinking attentively, creating ways to gratify the stomach, then we cannot claim that gastronomy is a modern invention, as has often been said.

SEVEN

The Beautiful and the Good

The making of colors

"The eye also wants its share" is something we have often heard when looking at a dish artfully arranged and decorated, meaning that one eats not with the mouth alone but with the eyes, and other senses as well. That is why colors have always been important in defining the appeal of food, today as yesterday. However, the role they played in the kitchens of the past (the Middle Ages, the Renaissance, the Baroque) was not the same as it is today.

Today color serves primarily to enhance the naturalness and freshness of the product. A few centuries ago, on the contrary, color was regarded as an artifice, an addition, a painterly touch that modified the natural appearance of the food. For precisely that reason many accessory products were used in preparing dishes. White was obtained with rice flour, almond milk, or bread crumbs; green, from minced herbs; yellow, from saffron or egg yolk; black, blue, and violet, from wild fruits. Red, however, took time to appear on the palette of colors used by cooks. Not until the introduction of the tomato into European cooking, and not before the eighteenth century, did red become a major protagonist (and too much so).

Among the various colors the prize went for a long time to yellow, associated with sunlight, joy, and happiness. Which was why saffron met with such extraordinary success. In the cookbooks of the fifteenth and sixteenth centuries we see it used in astounding quantities: "This dish should be a deep yellow." Dozens of recipes end with this chromatic instruction. This was all the more important for festive dishes. In the Low Countries a dish of yellow rice was served to celebrate a wedding and was similar in appearance, if not in consistency, to the yellow rice that became the fashion in Milan. In a famous painting by Pieter Breughel, *A Country Wedding*, we see bowls of this yellow rice in the foreground (along with others containing a white gruel, symbol of immaculate purity).

The yellow of saffron evoked an even more precious yellow, that of gold, which in those centuries reigned over Italian and Flemish figurative art. Saffron represented the gastronomic version of that gold, although some recipes actually included the precious metal (which, as late as the twentieth century, was proposed by Gualtiero Marchesi as a decoration on his famous "reworking" of risotto alla milanese).[1] This, evidently, is not and was not within the means of everyone, but an old Flemish proverb guarantees that he who is content with saffron rice on this earth will, in Paradise, be able to savor a dish made entirely of gold.

White or red?

A summer evening in a fish restaurant on the Adriatic coast. As a first course we can choose among tagliolini, strozzapreti, gnocchi, ravioli. For the sauce there are two options, white or red, otherwise dry.

Not really surprising, and yet never before that evening, faced with the need to choose between red and white, had I ever clearly seen that the tomato is one of those things that divide the world in two. Like chocolate. Years before, in a Spanish restaurant, when it came time for dessert we were asked if we wanted it with or without chocolate, and that time as well the same thought occurred to me.

---

[1] Chef-owner of the three-star restaurant in Milan.

Everyone has his own taste and all tastes are to be respected, but there are important limitations, tastes that determine our choices. There are "basic" tastes that often have nothing to do with the principal ingredient of a dish but are related to those that would seem to be secondary. Do we prefer a *soffritto*[2] with garlic or with onions? These are precisely the aromatic ingredients that give a recipe its tone, that assure its identity, its personality.

Tomato sauce entered into our cooking only recently. Its first appearance goes no farther back than the end of the seventeenth century. Two centuries had elapsed from the time the red (or yellow) *Solanum lycopersicum* first reached Europe from America. Its use as a sauce, already known in the New World, first took hold in Spain, to such a degree that for some time it was called the Spanish sauce in Italy. (It appears under this name in the cookbook by Antonio Latini, published in Naples in 1692–94.) Tomato sauce slowly found its place among the many sauces that were typical of Italian cuisine ever since the Middle Ages: the perennial accompaniment to meat and fish. Then, at the beginning of the nineteenth century, the tomato met pasta and changed its color.

Many sauces were named for the color their ingredients bestowed on them: green, white, camel-colored (extremely famous during the Middle Ages; a brownish color produced by cinnamon on a white ground). Among the many sauces—to which cookbooks devoted special attention and entire chapters—a red one was missing. The tomato finally filled the void by enfranchising this color, endowing it with all the rights and privileges of the world of gastronomy.

Pasta, in particular, which for centuries had been steadfastly white, sauced only with butter and cheese and perhaps a pinch of pepper, veered decidedly toward red. Other colors—yellow and green above all—remained supporting actors. The ultimate choice became white or red.

---

[2] A basic preparation in Mediterranean dishes of onions and/or garlic sautéed in oil.

Carrot red

The fascination of the carrot is in large part its color, unusual and original, a color, what is more, that changed over time. The orange color that today seems normal was achieved through crossbreeding in the seventeenth century, perfected by Dutch horticulturists to honor the royal family, the House of Orange. In ancient and medieval times the carrot was darker and tended toward the purple-red, still seen today in a few local varieties. This explains why an agronomist of the fifteenth century, Corniolo della Cornia, called it "red parsnip," seeing it almost as a colored variant of the parsnip, a white root vegetable widely used in cooking at the time. Doctors today explain that it is precisely by its color that the nutritional qualities of a plant are recognized, and they recommend that our daily diet include red, purple, or orange foods. The relation between colors and flavors (the latter considered the expression and instrument of the nutritional value of a food) was already suggested by Aristotle, who, in *De anima*, set up a complex system of correspondences between principal colors and flavors: white corresponds to sweet, red to sour. . . .

Sour was the flavor of the carrot, according to ancient writers, sour, but leaning toward sweet. The best carrots, in the opinion of the physician Castor Durante da Gualdo, are the big sweet ones—a characteristic that farmers of the Modern Era progressively emphasized, thereby slowly modifying the "wild" nature of the plant. Along with its taste, its color was also modified. If Costanzo Felici, still in the sixteenth century, spoke only of carrots "with their lovely vermilion color," which he recommends using in salads after having boiled them or cooked them under embers, at the start of the next century Giocomo Castelvetro was among the first to write about "red and yellow" carrots.

In any case, for a long time it was not the flavor but the color of carrots that was appreciated in cooking. In cookbooks of the medieval period they appear almost exclusively as ingredients for a *colored compote,* like the "Lombard compote," archetype of the *mostarda* from Cremona,—[3] which contains various kinds of fruits and vegetables. Corniolo della Cornia writes that the carrot "reddens the turnip in the compote"—a concoction that would seem to be more decorative than gustatory but that we would be mistaken to regard as merely accessory in a culture that, in the wake of Aristotle and medical-dietary thinking, long believed that the pairing of colors and flavors, appearance and taste, was fundamental. It does not seem any different today.

The search for beauty is not a futile exercise but a primary need for humans. The color of plants attracts us for that as well. The orange or red of carrots is beautiful and good, good *because* it is beautiful.

Culinary artifices

Bologna, January 1487. Annibale II Bentivoglio, first-born of Giovanni II, lord of Bologna, returns to the city with young Lucrezia, daughter of Ercole, duke of Ferrara; she had been married to Annibale by proxy some ten years earlier. For the occasion, great festivities were planned with balls, jousts, music, games, and a sumptuous banquet. The chronicler Cherubino Ghirardacci has left us a detailed account of this event in his descriptions of the scintillating choreography, the convivial rituals, the dishes that were served. Among many astounding things are the marvelous *artifices* that the palace cooks dreamed up and realized. In Ghirardacci's text the word *artifice* reappears constantly. At first with less importance, merely to describe the "artificial water," meaning perfumed water that was offered to the guests at the beginning of the banquet to rinse their hands. Then, to describe a castle made of sugar "very artfully constructed," that was brought into the hall during the first course, filled with birds that at a given moment were let loose and flew around to the "great pleasure and delight"

---

[3] A condiment of sweet pickled fruit.

of the guests. Later the meat dishes began to arrive—roasted, boiled, stewed, encased in pastry—all with the same remarkable characteristic: "all the animals and birds brought to the table that had previously been cooked were so artfully arranged and decorated with their feathers and their skins that they looked alive." With great skill, the cooks prepared the animals in such a way that they seemed to be still living—a trick bordering on the macabre, which the culture and the taste of the time enjoyed enormously. Artifice, fabrication, imitation were much appreciated. What was appreciated was the idea of man imitating and at the same time manipulating nature, making things seem different from what they are. An analogous principle led to modifying, at times distorting the natural flavors, colors, and consistencies of products.

There was an "artificial castle," obviously made of sugar, filled with rabbits that came out running in all directions while at the table rabbit pies were being served. Then another one, this time with "a huge pig" inside (out of prudence, this animal was not set loose). At the end of the banquet, each of the illustrious guests received a sugar sculpture with symbols of his city or family, all made "with such artistry and artifice that each one of them seemed no small marvel."

The evening ended with fireworks, "ingeniously set off in the middle of the piazza . . . where many imitation snakes held up a huge ball filled with imitation tubes of cannon powder." We are still very fond of sparkling wheels and other firework displays, but this is perhaps the only *artifice* that continues to provide us with pleasurable astonishment. Modern culture has progressively rediscovered (in cooking as well) the value of *natural* things, and views the artificial in mostly negative terms. When values change, the meaning of words also changes.

Compositions and compotes

"Compote," from the Latin *componere*, to put together, is the culinary variant of terms that evoke the idea of construction, invention, artifice. Just as a literary composition puts words together, moves them around and reassembles them into a poem or a novel; just as a musical composition puts notes together, moves them around and reassembles them into a song or a symphony, so a compote puts certain ingredients together, separates them and remixes them to make a gastronomic specialty. You take fruit (this is usually the basic product); cut it; mix it with sweet, salty, spicy flavors; cook it slowly; and recompose it, giving it a new meaning, a taste it did not have before. You re-create it, invent a new use for it to accompany, enhance, season other dishes.

In the Italian tradition, the oldest examples of a compote[4] are to be found in recipes from the late Middle Ages. A text from the fifteenth century describes how to make *chomposte buone*, good compotes, of turnips, carrots, and pears. The recipe begins with cooking carrots after having washed them thoroughly, "and when they begin to smell cooked," take them out of the water and let them dry. The turnips are cooked separately, to which, after a while, the pears are added. In the meantime, to the water in which the carrots cooked, add cabbage, celery root, parsley, and parsnip. Then let everything dry on a tablecloth for a day and a night, after which cut everything as you like, according to the way you want the compote to look, "and put everything that was sliced into good vinegar," letting it soak for three days. Now the *mostarda* is almost ready, diluted in cooked wine with the addition of *sapa* (a concentration of cooked must) along with pepper, ginger, cinnamon, and coriander, all well ground together [in a mortar]. A pinch of saffron, also diluted in wine, will make "the *chomposte* turn all yellow." When this *savore*, or sauce, is "arranged in order" (which beautifully expresses the idea of a masterpiece being constructed), you take the cut turnips, pears, and carrots, along with the rest that has macerated in vinegar, and layer them in a pan, after having sprinkled the bottom with fennel and raisins. Each layer has to be alternated with an

---

[4] More commonly known in English as a relish, and as *mostarda* in Italian today..

identical layer of the sauce, and each one sprinkled with fennel and raisins, and grated horseradish, as well as "a fair amount of salt" added to the *mostarda*. "And may it be good."

Medieval and Renaissance gastronomy was very interested in dishes of this kind, which enjoyed particular prestige on the table of the powerful. The use of humble ingredients, like carrots and turnips, immediately acquired a different connotation when enriched with precious spices unavailable to ordinary people. The very complexity of the preparation—even if only implied in a recipe like the one above—contributed to endowing these *chomposte* with the sophistication of an exclusive product, the result of a difficult and delicate concoction, more like the product of a chemical laboratory than a kitchen. Not by chance did the celebrated Nostradamus, himself a doctor and an alchemist, publish in 1556 a work devoted to the preparation of compotes,[5] understood by him as the more generic category of *confetture,* jams—the two terms, which tend to become confused, do have a similar meaning. Like *componere* [to compose], *conficere* [to fabricate] evokes the idea of artifice, elaboration born of human inventiveness.

If cooking is the modification of the order of the world and the nature of things, thereby imposing on them identities different from their natural ones, then a compote is the perfect metaphor for this kind of exciting process.

Confetti (sugarcoated almonds, spices, etc.)

I was in Flavigny, in Burgundy. The major gastronomic attraction of this charming village (where "Chocolat" was filmed) is the little factory, located on the grounds of the medieval abbey founded in the eighth century by the monk Widerard, where sugared confections are made. It would seem that already in 1591, visiting guests

---

[5] Relishes or jams.

were offered "anise of Flavigny," perhaps invented by those monks: anise seeds covered with so many layers of sugar syrup that they turned into a small round confection, like those that are made in the factory today, where some twenty people perpetuate a centuries-old tradition.

Confetti are a medieval invention, devised in a pharmaceutical setting and only later transferred to the domain of gastronomy. The term (from the Latin *conficere*, to fabricate) indicates that it was something artificial not found in nature, an invention, precisely. The idea was to sweeten medicinal substances (herbs, spices, seeds) to make them more palatable, easier to swallow: "Just a spoonful of sugar makes the medicine go down," in the words of a familiar song. It was not only to "accompany" the substance contained in the confection: The sugar itself, which only spread throughout Europe at the end of the Middle Ages, was held to be beneficial for the organism in its function as the bearer of sweetness—the perfect flavor and exemplar of a balanced and proper nutriment. If the sugar included a spice, held in turn to promote good digestion (since it provided heat to the stomach, aiding the digestive process, which was understood as the physical mechanism for "cooking" food), nothing could be better. The spice is good, the sugar is good, the *confetto* is excellent. The custom of serving spiced *confetti* at the end of a meal took root in Italy during the closing centuries of the Middle Ages and continued throughout the Renaissance. Both sugar and spices were then the mark of a noble table; the *confetto* was doubly so.

Spiced confetti could be enriched with various aromas and perfumes. In Flavigny today they are made with the flavors of orange, mint, licorice, rose, violet. The classic ones are those with anise, and it is a pleasure to discover the little seed at the end of a long and elaborate meal. Care must be taken not to chew too quickly; the seed might disappear from the tongue. One should not be in a hurry when savoring a confetto, for to find the seed requires attention and concentration. This constraint of slowness is almost an exercise in relaxation, itself useful for predisposing the body to a state of well-being.

Beauty is not a superfluous benefit

When eating, all the senses are in play. The Chinese tradition maintains that for a food to be perfect, it has to stimulate all of them. The sense of smell is almost one with that of taste (the noted gastronome Brillat-Savarin called it "the sentinel of taste"), which is why a cold is enough to impair the taste of food. Then there is touch: To touch a food (salami, cheese) helps us taste it better, more fully. Hearing would seem to be more marginal, nonetheless, just to hear the sizzling of frying food already arouses our taste buds (not to mention the bubbling of champagne or Coca Cola). And finally, sight, also claims its part, as the oft-repeated adage assures us.

The beauty of food is thus not marginal to the gustatory experience. To define a food as beautiful does not mean reducing it to a visual object, or concentrating on secondary aspects of the table and of gastronomy. Beauty is a global experience that begins long before products become food; it comprises respect for the environment, attention to the growing places and seasons of plants, and gratitude to those who work the soil and provide us with food. Then there is attention to detail, the harmony of the event, the sincerity of the relationships that bring us together around the table. All of this is beauty, not as accessory but as necessity: the beauty of freshly picked fruit, the beauty of good health, of sharing, of honesty.

Beauty is not the privilege of the few. It is a primary need of the individual and of society. Beauty is natural, but it has to be cultivated and is therefore also culture. Beauty makes things more acceptable, more pleasing, more desirable. The ancient Greeks thought that the body and the spirit were fundamentally the same and that a truly beautiful man could not be other than truly good, which is why they coined the expression *kalòs kai agathòs*, beautiful and good, to be understood as a hendiadys—one concept that holds two.

And so it is for food. To be really good it has to be really beautiful. Not only the rich food of grand occasions, but even humble, ordinary, daily food. Beauty is needed every day.

EIGHT

Convivial Rituals

The call of the wild (around the barbecue)

The barbecue is very much in fashion. I have read that in the United States alone, electric, gas, charcoal grills, and every kind of accessory (forks, spatulas, pincers, skewers, basting brushes) that go with this primordial ritual represent a four-billion-dollar business. The contradiction is obvious. On the one hand, the most sophisticated technological implements are used. On the other, barbecuing celebrates the simplicity of an archaic gesture going back to the first humans who, once fire was domesticated, made it the instrument of simple food, a world away from the sophisticated complexities that in time would enliven the culinary arts. It is this archaic dimension of our alimentary history that is revived by the ritual of the barbecue. Because a ritual it is, no more no less. The inviting aroma of grilling meat is not only a celebration of taste; the strong odor of coals is not only a delicacy for the initiated. There is something more, something that one is tempted to label "the call of the wild."

This ritual is totally carnivorous. Tomatoes and eggplant may take part, and there is no lack of fanciful suggestions for grilling all kinds of food, even pasta. They are irrelevant, however, and do not alter the deep-rooted identity of grilling. It is not hard to conceive of it as the concluding moment of a hunting party, such as the ones that provided our ancestors with food.

The magical moment for barbecuing is summertime, when the warmth of evening invites us out, into a patio or garden, park or woods. This is not only a contingency of climate but the primordial condition of the ritual. Grilling takes place in a particular space that, wherever it may be, has to be in the open—outside the house, the kitchen, the domesticity of pots and the water that boils in them. The space of grilling is that of an open fire, the wild space of the forest, evoked by any possible surrogates, even if only the terrace of a high-rise apartment building; what matters is being outside.

These cultural implications are not always explicit nor even conscious. What is explicit and conscious is the summons to conviviality, to friendship, to the gesture of sharing in the preparation and consumption of food. This collective dimension has always been part of the social ritual of a meal as a symbol of the group, of its cohesion, of the solidarity that goes into the effort of procuring food and in the pleasure of consuming it together. The desire for company that seems to be the initial motivation for gathering guests at a barbecue today generally occurs during the free time of a weekend, but the image of togetherness that it evokes has always been present in human life. The ritual of survival cannot be celebrated by oneself.

A masculine ritual

When it comes to barbecuing, the preparation of food tends to change gender. If our history of food has placed woman at the center of the domestic kitchen, the grill and the rotisserie are by definition a masculine enterprise. Of course, it was she who cooked the chicken as only she knows how to make it, and eggplant and tomatoes were never burned; they were perfect. Inevitably, it was he behind her, he who started the fire and never tired of giving unwanted advice. At other times it was he and he alone who was master of the game, tamer of the flame, self-styled expert of "the right timing." This inversion of roles is the distinctive mark of the grill. The grill substitutes the outside for the inside, open space for the house. It substitutes the hunter for the woman who domesticates the food and prepares it in the kitchen. It brings the "cultural" creation of the kitchen back to "nature," real or pretended, which knew nothing of techniques and implements, which ignored the art of cuisine and was satisfied with merely cooking food.

Without pots, without pans, without water, without oil, with only the aid of fire and a piece of metal to hold the raw meat, the act of cooking regains the primordial sense that it must have had when Prometheus first offered fire to humanity. Every human culture has occasional nostalgia for that past, more mythical than real; every culture wants to complete itself with the nature from which it presumes it was separated.

Even this "nature" is a cultural construct. It is impossible to tend the fire, the flame, the heat, without patient study, without a practical knowledge that is learned and is taught. The man of the forest, who hunts and cooks his prey, is not exactly the "wild" man described in ancient and medieval texts, and represented in frescoes and popular prints, protagonist of legends still vivid in our mountain regions. Legends, moreover, that reveal the ambiguity regarding the moment when "wild" man is presumed to have invented "civilization." It is he, in so many stories, who taught humans the methods of farming and animal husbandry, the secret of ceramics, the art of cooking.

It is this myth that is more or less consciously relived in the ritual of the barbecue: the preparation of food outside the house, simply, without encumbrances, without the weight of "civilization." If it is true that civilization was made by women, in this instance they will have to stand aside.

Rucola in the White House

In the fall of 2008, when the presidential campaign was raging in America, the Republican candidate, John McCain, was invited to a popular food channel, one of the many that fill television screens on either side of the Atlantic. He donned an apron and explained his method for preparing spare ribs: His "secret" is to let them marinate for ten hours in pepper and garlic before putting them on the grill. McCain also assured the audience that once elected, one of his first acts would be to set up a large barbecue in the garden of the White House. A great publicity stunt, since a barbecue in the garden is the preferred cooking technique of every self-respecting American, a gastronomic myth that is celebrated every weekend, when friends are invited to eat ribs and hamburgers not terribly different from those eaten during the week in restaurants. The presidential candidate intended to reaffirm his Americanism in this manner, his participation in the culture and traditions of the land.

Every myth contains values and symbols that go beyond the concrete and "technical" dimensions of the gesture. Cooking spare ribs on a barbecue at home is not just for eating but also, and perhaps mostly, for identifying oneself as native to a culture, like the American one, deeply marked by the myth of the outdoors, of eating in the midst of nature, of the strong, hearty man who does not waste time fussing in the kitchen (in fact, the barbecue, like the spit, is almost always a "guy thing"). To announce that a barbecue will be installed in the White House garden is an effective way of reassuring a certain type of voter, generally masculine and generally conservative, that the traditional values of the American people will be left unchanged.

We know how that ended. John McCain did not move into the White House and no barbecue showed up in the garden. Instead, the new inhabitant of the White House is a young African-American who, in an interview, said that he liked salads with rucola[1] and parmesan. This too is a declaration pregnant with symbolic meaning. It is "light" and dynamic, more oriented toward the

---

[1] Known in America as arugula, its southern Italian pronunciation.

Mediterranean than to America, to immigrants rather than to Yankees. Obama's salad is in a way provocative, because it implies change with regard to the culture of the barbecue.

We now know that Mrs. Obama has planted a vegetable garden behind the White House.

Christmas dinner

The table has always been the ideal place to celebrate a holiday. Communal dining and a groaning table are a ritual that tighten the bonds of the group and stave off the fear of hunger. If this applies to any banquet and any holiday, it is all the more valid for Christmas, a celebration of birth and the beginning of life. The pagan tradition celebrated the winter solstice, which marked the return of the sun and of nature. The Christian liturgy, by superimposing itself on the earlier cults, wanted to establish, precisely in that period of the year, the birth of Christ, interpreted as "the new sun" and as the beginning of "the new life."

Among the ritual foods of the Christmas holiday, a particular symbolic meaning is to be found in sweet breads containing seeds, candied fruits, and raisins, all representing fertility and prosperity. Great feasts, however, are primarily the triumph of meat, perhaps for the sacrificial significance of meat ever since antiquity, or, more simply, because for centuries meat was the principal food desire of humans, the most frustrated and most difficult to satisfy, especially among the less well-to-do. The endemic hunger for meat (which corresponded to a truly excessive consumption by the upper classes) was exorcized by exaggerated consumption on feast days, which temporarily equalized the eating habits of rich and poor.

On the day of the holiday it was not enough to eat great quantities of meat. It was necessary to display it, and conspicuously. Goethe, during his travels in Italy in 1787, wrote from Naples: "For Christmas the city becomes a kind of Land of Cockaigne. All along the streets garlands of food are hung and crowns of sausages tied with red ribbons can be seen. Turkeys all have a red banderole attached to their tail. I have been told that 30,000 of them have been sold, not counting those fattened privately in homes. In the meantime, a large number of donkeys laden with greens, capons and kids trot around the city and the market." Everybody is eating copiously, particularly meat, but that does not suffice: Everybody has to know how much, because every ritual, to be meaningful, has to be shared and communicated. "Each year," Goethe continues, "an official from the police rides through the city on horseback, accompanied by a trumpeter, and announces in the squares and at crossroads how many thousands of steer, calves, kids, lambs, pigs the Neapolitans have eaten. The people are overjoyed to hear these huge numbers, and each person remembers with satisfaction how much he contributed to the pleasure." Officials and trumpeters to proclaim loudly how much we have eaten, how remarkable we were! We would be hard put to find a more fitting image of the symbolism of these food orgies that drive away hunger and augur plenty.

What if Christmas falls on a Friday, a day dedicated to moderate eating and abstinence from meat? Which will prevail, the obligation of penance or that of celebrating the holiday with a memorable feast? Saint Francis had no doubts about this question. When his disciples, as related by Tommaso da Celano, discussed this prickly problem among themselves, and then, still undecided, sent brother Morico to ask the master, they received an unequivocal response: "You sin, brother, to call Friday[2] the day the Child was born to us. On a day like that I would want even the walls to eat meat, but since that is impossible, let them at least be spread with it on the outside." Saint Francis, his biographer went on to explain, was particularly devoted to Christmas and "wanted poor people and beggars to be stuffed full by the rich, and oxen and donkeys to receive a ration of food and hay more copious than usual." He is reputed

---

[2] Meaning a day of abstinence.

to have said to his companions, "If I ever manage to speak to the emperor, I will beg him to issue an edict that requires of everyone who has the means to scatter wheat and grain along the streets so that on a day of such solemnity, the birds, and particularly the sister larks will have food in abundance." This image of Christmas as a universal holiday becomes a kind of cosmic banquet that brings together all the creatures of the universe, rich people and poor people, animals on the ground and birds in the air, all the way to walls, if only they were able to participate.

Even today, in a society of assured consumption, too often to excess, does it still makes sense to celebrate the holiday with a ritual feast? One would say no. New attitudes toward food, more relaxed or even detached, have replaced the old obsessions, and this is surely not regrettable. Nonetheless, something is worth keeping. The holiday can be an occasion for greater attention to food, for even formal treatment of the convivial event, for a moment's reflection on the good fortune of being able to choose the foods we like, and on the respect due the work, the techniques, the skills that produce the good things we eat.

A hundred cappelletti

According to Pellegrino Artusi, the father of Italian cuisine, Christmas dinner should consist of six courses. The first can only be broth with a particular kind of pasta in it, in honor of the traditions of his native region: "cappelletti as served in Romagna."[3] This is followed, as "starters" (in Italian we would call these antipasti, but in the Artusian system they follow the opening broth), by crostini.[4] Then, three meat dishes: boiled (capon, "with a mold of green rice"), cold (hare in pastry) and roasted ("guinea hen and game birds"). For

---

[3] A small, filled, envelope-style pasta, rather than the doughnut shape of tortellini.
[4] Chicken liver paste on grilled bread slices.

dessert he proposes a choice of *Sienese panforte*,[5] and *pane cer-tosina* [a sweet oval bread native to Bologna, made with candied fruit, almonds, dark chocolate, raisins, anise seeds, and cinnamon] and toasted almond ice cream.

In this menu, cappelletti and capon are understood as insepa-rably yoked. This dish, Artusi explains in the related recipe that triumphantly opens the chapter on pasta in broth, "to be more appealing to the taste, requires a broth made from capon, that diminished animal[6] which generously offers itself in celebration of Christmas as a sacrifice to humanity." Relating the customs of his native Romagna, he evokes the exploits of certain "heroes" who "on the said day [of Christmas] pride themselves on having eaten one hundred cappelletti."

The epic of great eaters has been for centuries a hallowed theme in popular tradition, recorded in many literary works. In the six-teenth century, the Milanese Ortensio Lando entertained himself by writing a veritable catalog of "immoderate eaters"; Giulio Cesare Croce, in the seventeenth, invented a mythical Gian Diluvio da Trippaldo, the perfect "hyperbole of the Emilian eater," as defined by Piero Camporesi; and there is hardly any need to recall Gar-gantua, Rabelais's famous character, whose very name carries the image of an open gullet. Popular imagination has always regarded these champions having the capacity of eating prodigiously, and the possibility of so doing, with admiration and reverence. Those heroes were the vindicators of an unappeased appetite, of a daily life too often spent in misery, of an unsatisfied desire to eat bet-ter and more. Important holidays, like Christmas, were the ideal occasion to hope for an abundance of food by indulging in excess and exaggerated display. The hundred cappelletti of the Artusian heroes are a boast that reflects the world of hunger like a mirror.

---

[5] A dense, round confection, rather than a bread, of candied fruit and almonds, a specialty of Siena.

[6] Capon is a castrated rooster.

Granted, eating like that, as Artusi observes, "is a way to croak, which happened to someone I know." Happy the country, we would add, in the words of Bertolt Brecht, that has no need of heroes.

Carnival and Lent

Carnival is a word that has a strange destiny. It evokes feasting, abundance, even excess and debauchery, whereas its etymology suggests the opposite. The word, in fact, is of medieval origin and derives from *carnelevare*, meaning "to take meat away," in other words, restricting the diet, doing penance, mortifying the body by at least denying it some of the pleasure that food can provide. "Carnival" is the practice of eliminating meat and other food of animal origin during the Lenten period, the forty days that precede Easter. Imposed by the church calendar as of the fifth to sixth centuries, abstinence from food was intended to signify the participation of the faithful in the suffering of Christ on the cross, and to demonstrate, by means of this denial, personal commitment to the Christian community. In that period butchers closed their shops while fishmongers made a fortune, unless (as happened in certain cities) those very butchers recycled themselves as purveyors of fish. The term *carnival*, which indicated the passage from a meat diet to a meatless diet, was used at one point to signal the last day of merriment, with Mardi Gras preceding the onset of Lent, and by extension the entire period that ended with that day. This marked an opposition between Carnival and Lent, which was represented in literature (there was even a genre, starting in the Middle Ages, known as "the battle between Lent and Carnival") as well as in figurative works, such as the famous painting by Breughel.

The first example of a "battle" is a French text of the third century, in which foods of abstinence (*magro,* lean) and foods of feasting (*grasso,* fat) fight in opposing armies. On one side, fish, on the other, meat, supported by eggs and dairy products. Roast capons clash with whitings, flounder and mackerel with beef, eel with pork sausage. Vegetables fight on both sides, depending on how they are prepared: peas in oil on one side, those in lard on the other. The story, filled with detailed strategies of attack and defense, ends with the victory of Carnival and the surrender of Lent, which, to make peace, agrees to limit its presence on the territory to a few weeks a year. In the end one understands that the battle was a sham, because the territory (that is, the duration of a year) had already been divided in advance.

Lenten diet, gastronomic discoveries

Why do the rules for Lenten abstinence have meat as their objective? Why precisely *that* sacrifice?

In the Middle Ages, meat was held to be the greatest alimentary pleasure, the food most capable of satisfying the needs and desires of the body. "Meat nourishes and fattens humans more than any other food," wrote the doctors (Aldobrandino of Siena, for example, along with many others). *La carne nutre la carne* [meat nourishes flesh] Christian moralists repeated, with a clever and striking play on words. However, the renunciation of this desire was seen as the prime form of alimentary penance and the prime symbol of approaching spiritual aspirations. The diet required by the liturgical calendar during Lent—but also during other periods of the year and on particular days of the week—could nonetheless be delicious. Choice fish and delicate vegetables could easily replace meat on the determined days. An entire literature ironizes on the delicacies that were passed off as Lenten practices. Pierre Abelard, the twelfth-century philosopher, asked what merit there could be in renouncing everyday meat to have highly expensive fish. The point is that it was a *substitution*. The consumption of fish was not dictated, at least not at first, by a choice of taste, but rather by an obligation, a restriction, an imposed renunciation. For this reason, "lean" foods acquired low social standing (fish and vegetables in oil, to which dairy products were added in the late Middle Ages and remained excluded except on days of total abstinence). The resistance, still today, to "lean" foods, starting with fish and vegetables, can be explained historically by their long association with obligatory consumption. Their inferior status is reflected even in the relatively successful attempts to imitate "fat" foods, as evidenced by cookbooks written between the Middle Ages and the Modern Era.

This does not negate the fact that Lenten requirements did indeed open the way to new gastronomic initiatives. The most outstanding example is pasta, which took its place in medieval and Renaissance cookbooks as "lean" food. The multiplicity of preparations and recipes that were developed to fulfill liturgical requirements opened new chapters in the history of food and cooking. During the seventeenth and eighteenth centuries, when the fat/lean alternative was no longer the order of the day, and recipes for fish and vegetables began to lose their Lenten stamp, the innumerable "obligatory" experiments undertaken to make meatless dishes appetizing proved to be an unexpected investment in gastronomic culture.

Easter eggs

In all cultures, Easter (like similar events that recur at the onset of spring) is the celebration of rebirth. In a religious context this notion enters into the sphere of the sacred. The Hebraic tradition recalls the rebirth of the Chosen People who escaped slavery in Egypt; Christianity celebrates the resurrection of Christ and the redemption of humanity. What is evident is the relationship between these traditions, along with a subtext of nature worship related to the cycles of nature. It is the celebration of nature, reborn after the "death" of winter.

Easter too, like all major and minor anniversaries, is celebrated with a festive banquet. The meal, the sharing of food carefully prepared and dictated by ritual, is always the principal way of marking the holiday. In the particular case of Easter, the Christian tradition takes up certain themes that come from the Hebraic tradition, like lamb. However, it is the ancient "naturalistic" culture that presides over the choice of the egg as the quintessential food symbol of this holiday. The egg is the life that reproduces itself, that is reborn. The blessing of eggs is the crucial moment of the traditional Christian ritual. Foods based on eggs, like the *torta pasqualina*, Easter torte[7] can be found in various local traditions. The chocolate egg as well—altering the nature of the food and transferring it to the realm of sweet—recalls this ancient symbolism. The surprise inside, which cannot be missed, is the symbolic representation of the embryo, the "fertility" of this food.

Breakfast

You say "breakfast," and that seems obvious to you. Obvious that one should have it, in that way, and at that hour. Then you rethink this and you realize that many are the ways: bacon and sausages, cheese and eggs, flakes of cereal, yogurt, fresh and dried fruit, buttered toast and jam, even herring in Scandinavian countries. Buffets in good hotels are almost an anthology of breakfast, at least in the West. As a beverage, anything is possible: hot milk and cold fruit juice, coffee, tea, not to mention water or even wine. What about Africa, or Asia? Every culture has its own breakfast, nor is it said that one must have breakfast. How many people continue to have nothing but coffee, and no one is astonished? The range of possibilities seems almost infinite. Individual tastes and choices in this rite of passage from night to day only heighten the unpredictability of this rite.

It can be said that all alimentary customs grow out of a culture and therefore vary in time and space, along with personal options. Breakfast even more so, because the very idea of breakfast

---

[7] Made with chard, ricotta, and hard-boiled eggs.

is far from obvious. In the ancient world there seems to have been no specific way of thinking about it, no name for referring to it. Among the meals of the day, breakfast does not have a precise identity. There are no particular foods or beverages to qualify it. If anything, there are modalities of taking it that define it negatively with regard to main meals. Breakfast can be had standing instead of sitting, alone rather than with others. One thinks of breakfast standing at the bar of a café, without speaking, and a thread of continuity can be glimpsed, even if, to be truthful, breakfast at the bar is not without a certain convivial dimension. Especially if one is alone, a cup of coffee and a croissant or a doughnut can also be a way of sharing this activity with others, however impersonal or silent. The difficulty that doctors and dietitians encounter, even today, when they explain the importance of having a proper breakfast to meet the caloric intake of the day in a balanced way, is by itself proof that it is not a standard practice.

Nothing in the life and culture of human beings is obvious, nor can anything be taken for granted.

When snacking kills the snack[8]

The diminutive *merendina* suggests diminishing, lightening, repositioning; in a sense, de-ritualizing. The historic institution of the *merenda,* which traditionally fell at the half-way mark of the morning and of the afternoon during work and study time—the well-deserved refreshment, *merenda* from the Latin *mereo*, signifying "that which one should deserve"—has left room for a smaller, less important *merendina* that minimizes the significance of the event,

---

[8] The title of this section is "When *merendine* kill the *merenda.*" The Italian *merenda* has no English equivalent. The French have a *goûter,* when children come home from school; the English have elevenses and tea-time. In America one has a snack, or a coffee break, but these words do not connote the official pause for refreshment that has been practiced in Italy for centuries.

its temporal and spatial placement. It is insignificant in the literal sense: an event that does not signify, does not express, does not communicate social import—the time of repose and refreshment after a period of work or study—but, freed from the rhythm of the day, is reduced to the object of the refreshment (a little snack) taken out of its context. Since the time frame of the *merenda* is no longer involved, what remains is a *merendina* to be consumed. The message of the food industry is clear: I am the snack, I can be eaten whenever you like. Time is no longer a factor, the *merendina* can now extend throughout the day, can even replace a meal for those who do not have the time, or for those who delude themselves into believing they are thereby cutting calories. The idea of a pause remains, but it is a pause that can occur at any moment. It only takes a contraction of the stomach and the hand goes out, the snack is ready, hunger is placated. The food-object has replaced the food-event.

Along with time, space has disappeared. The *merenda*, like lunch or dinner, had clearly defined locations for its consumption. During the school morning, you went outside for some air, in the corridor, the courtyard, the garden. In the middle of the afternoon, having returned home from school, a little meal awaited you, quick but only seemingly informal: bread, jam, butter, chocolate, milk, fruit juice. . . . The location could be the kitchen, the living room, the garden: but there *was* a location. The eat-and-run *merendina* has no location. It can be grabbed and downed anywhere, in one's seat at school, in the office, in the street, in front of television; in other words, while doing something else, in places designated for other purposes.

Dietitians will tell us all about the merits and demerits of snacking: Some will be nostalgic for the old bread and jam, others will intelligently choose among the products, not all of them equal, that the food industry invents and proposes from time to time. It is not just a matter of calories, sugar or carbohydrates. The factors that deserve attention are primarily time and space, the natural dimensions of our life, which, on close inspection, are not natural at all, but are always culturally determined according to parameters, perspectives and interests that are never equally important. I would make a little comment, as I often do, about the words: The snack is always at arm's reach; it is no longer something deserved, but is something due you, something taken for granted, of minimal affective worth. The *merendina* kills the *merenda*.

Silence, we're eating

Conversation (preferably not loud) would seem to be a natural attribute of mealtime. Men, Aristotle wrote, are "social animals" who like to do things in company. Even the act of eating is preferably experienced with others, and conversation is generally an essential component. This explains why Plutarch devoted one of his "questions" (in the *Roman and Greek Questions* of the *Moralia)* to what is or is not suitable for discussion while eating, what subjects may or may not be brought to the table. However, when we think of the medieval monastic rules imposing silence during meals, we are confronted with an anomaly, an unnatural norm that indicates a difference between the monk's table and that of "others," between his way of life and the worldly life.

In the refectory the monk must keep silence, and while eating must listen to edifying texts read out loud: biblical passages, lives of the saints, precepts of monastic life, parts of the anthologies, *Collationes,* assembled by Giovanni Cassiano, which led to the association of the term *colazione* with mealtime.[9] The obligation of silence led to curious situations. Some communities figured out ways to observe the requirement without giving up communication. Is it possible to speak without speaking? Apparently it is. Words are not necessary to communicate. All kinds of signs, hand and body gestures, winks were invented to say what one wished

---

[9] In modern Italian, *colazione* is a light lunch; breakfast is *prima colazione.*

without disobeying the Rule. The Cluniac monasteries, those that grew out of the Benedictine abbey of Cluny in Burgundy, devised a veritable "silent language," endowed with a rudimentary dictionary and an elementary grammar. At first this was practiced secretly and illicitly (like signals between bridge partners); later, it was accepted and even codified in writing. In the eleventh century, lists of "signs" were included in the "practices" drawn up by the abbots of the various monasteries, as an adjunct to the Benedictine Rule.

This was not without opposition. Certain monastic orders, like the Carthusian, refused to adopt this practice, considering it improper. There were also scandalized descriptions, like the one by Gerard of Cambrai, who visited the Benedictines of Canterbury in 1180 and noticed that at meals the most absolute silence reigned in the refectory, but the monks "conversed" animatedly among themselves. Gerard says he had the impression of being in the midst of a theatrical performance, and comments that the use of the lips would have been much more dignified than that ridiculous gesturing.

What criteria determined those signs? First and foremost, the rule of imitation. One had to translate the object visually, describe it with a gesture. For example, a fish was represented by a waving movement of the hand, held vertically with the fingers together: "The hand simulates the movement of the fish in the water." The kind of fish was specified by an additional sign. For the lamprey, it was suggested to "imitate with a finger on the upper jaw the spots that this fish has under the eyes." For the cuttlefish, "separate the fingers widely and wiggle them," imitating the animal's movement in water.

In other cases, one reproduced the way a product was used. To indicate salt, the movement of the hand sprinkling salt on food was imitated. "Bring together the thumb and the tips of the fingers and, holding them together, move them two or three times, separating them from the thumb as though sprinkling salt on something." To indicate walnuts, one made the gesture of cracking them: "The sign for walnuts: Put your finger in your mouth and keep it between your teeth on the right side of the mouth, as though you were cracking a walnut between your teeth." For the pig, the gesture of slaughter was used: "Hit your forehead with your fist, since this is the way it is stunned."

Gastronomic specifications also came out of these charades, such as the various ways of cooking bread (in the oven, under embers, in water, in a pan), the different colors of wine, the many ways of cooking eggs. Composite dishes were indicated by their primary ingredients, as in the case of *fladones*, a savory pie filled with cheese or something else, typical of medieval gastronomy: "Starting with the usual signs for bread and cheese, bend all the fingers of one hand to make a hole, and place it on the top of the other hand," thereby imitating the form of a pie.

Subsequent suggestions allude to the "social" significance of foods, to their symbolic function rather than to their material appearance. To indicate a salmon or a sturgeon (a pre-eminently noble fish during the Middle Ages), one had to add to the customary sign for fish a second, incomprehensible, sign: "Place your fist under your chin, with the thumb raised." Because "in this way one indicates ostentation, and it is above all the ostentatious and the rich who eat these fish."

The many dozens of such signs provide us with precious information about the culinary and alimentary culture of the Middle Ages—thanks to the rule of silence.

Eating on the highway

A way of traveling is also a way of eating. If the modality of travel is an inquisitive itinerary, an interest in what comes along by chance, then food too will have many variants and will be a means of entering into contact with the realities and cultures that one comes across. If, instead, the trip has only a single purpose, interposing itself between the point of departure and the point of arrival, like a parenthesis, to be bypassed as quickly and painlessly as possible, then food will be no more than an inattentive pause.

The asphalt ribbon of a highway seems expressly made for this second mode of travel: a straight line to the destination, ignoring territories along the way, their attractions, their identity. The highway, by its very nature, would seem made to transmit the idea of indifference to local gastronomy. One eats only out of necessity, the way one stops for gas. On the highway, food is our gas, and gas is not rooted in any particular locality.

For a certain period in our history, the de-localization of food (its detachment from any ties with particular places) has been synonymous with modernity. Highway stopping places quickly adapted themselves to this idea, not only for logistical reasons (simplification of supplies, efficiency of chain distribution, reduction of time for preparation), but also for the satisfaction of a widespread demand to find everywhere the same things, to be independent of local customs. During the mid-1990s this kind of artificial world created for our use was the winning choice, the same one that determined the success of fast food.

Did this really represent modernity? Does it still? The answer can only be negative. Parallel with the process of globalization, contemporary society (almost out of a physical mechanism of action and reaction) has evolved a veritable myth of territory. Paradoxically, it is the industrial society that has come to interpret territory in a positive sense, overcoming the diffidence of traditional culture toward regionalism, regarded as a sign of alimentary and gastronomic poverty. Regionalism could not constitute a positive value in societies like the *ancien régime*, which classified food according to social differences. A territory, at least in theory, does not differentiate; it has rich and poor, gentry and peasants. A "geography of taste" has always existed, because food and cooking have always existed, inevitably conditioned by the territory, but this phenomenon has never enjoyed much prestige. "Geographic taste," the appreciation of local differences and characteristics, is the discovery of modern sensibility.

The infatuation with globalization has left the field open to diverse objectives, once marginalized but today sought after, to the point of faddism. An "in" restaurant today seeks not to eliminate but rather to emphasize the bond with the region and seasonality of products (the chef who goes to the market every morning is a myth typical of today). This, with all its ambiguities and contradictions (and even some frauds) is the orientation of current public dining. This is the most modern modernity.

Even the highway restaurant has not failed to become aware of this, rethinking, as of the last half-century, its own image and its own identity from a totally new perspective. The link with territory, seemingly at odds with the logic of highway travel, has been progressively regained. The recipes recommended in restaurants for travelers by car, the specialties proposed for purchase, continue, in many cases, to be prisoners of the industrial culture of de-localization, but in cases of more astute management (which started earlier outside of Italy), the stopping place has become an occasion for looking around, a kind of display window of what the surrounding region has to offer in dishes, products, wines. The flavor of global conformism has now entered into a lively dialogue with regional specialties, seasonal recipes, and local products.

Fast food and conviviality

November 8, 2000, a disturbing headline stood out on the front page of the daily newspaper *Avvenire:* "Hamburger? It is atheistic." This synthesizes (in the typically cursory manner of journalism) the concluding sallies of an interview with Massimo Salani, author of a book on the relationship between food and religion. Deprecating the growth of fast food, which would imply the "complete oblivion of the sacrality of food," Salani, pushed by his interviewer, attributes this phenomenon to the Protestant cultural model, which emphasizes the direct relationship between man and God, and disregards "the aspect of community, of sharing" in dining.

This statement aroused considerable interest. The next day, November 9, Orazio La Rocca in *La Repubblica* reprinted the text of the interview and entitled it "The excommunication of the hamburger. Theology versus McDonald's." He asks the opinion of Monsignor Domenico Sigalini, who comments: "It is not proper to speak of sin and discuss morality on the subject of the food one eats." Nonetheless, there is no doubt that fast food "tends to nullify everything, to eliminate direct contact with others because of speed, to destroy the meaning of family." A sidebar informs us that the Church has joined an already sizable horde of McDonald's enemies: environmentalists, gastronomes, unions, politicians.

The mass of arguments that has piled up on this subject requires that some order be made. In one column is the accusation that the multinational fast food industry ignores animal rights, respect for regions, dignity of workers, gastronomic quality. The other column lists the threat to conviviality, the incompatibility between the "system" of fast food and the culture of sharing. I will limit myself here to considering this last point and will admit to being astounded a few years ago by the results of a poll taken among devotees of fast food. To the query, "Why do you patronize this place?" the reply was, "To meet friends." While unexpected, the statement indicates the quest for conviviality in the only place financially affordable to young people short of money. Moreover, many of us have seen families at a McDonald's. That fast food tends to "destroy the meaning of family," or the desire to eat in company, seems very much open to question.

NINE

Table Practices and Manners

The fork and the hands

Finger food: This expression indicates today the practice of nibbling food with one's fingers instead of using the classic fork. It would seem to be a "fashionable" practice, which was described (in an article in *Repubblica Salute*, November 23, 2006) as a "new tendency" when a dietitian was questioned on its possible nutritional consequences. "In essence, this is a fashion," the dietitian confirmed, pointing out the advantages of increased familiarity with food that the tactile contact can provide, and the dangers of uncontrolled quantities and hasty chewing.

This "new tendency" reflects the most ancient way of taking food throughout human history. In Europe, the fork did not come into wide use until the eighteenth century, distancing food from the eater, creating a filter between food and man, a distance that until then would not have been desired. Only for slippery or scorching foods, like buttered pasta, was a fork used ever since the Middle Ages, almost out of necessity. For the rest, the hands were preferred, a real "physiological utensil" with which one grasped and savored meat, fish, vegetables, not to mention dried sausages and cheese which still today are taken directly from the cutting board.

The pleasure of food, Chinese wisdom teaches, is an experience that involves all the senses: taste, evidently, but also smell, sight, hearing, and not least, touch. For centuries this conviction was also held by Western culture and sensibility. For this reason the introduction of the fork was long and bitterly contested. In the second half of the seventeenth century, Vincenzo Nolfi wrote a treatise on etiquette for noble ladies in which he maintained that the fork was an instrument destined for rapid disappearance, since one's own hands "are less disgusting" than a piece of silver. By that he meant that meat, taken with a fork, did not taste of meat but of metal.

Hardly a "new tendency," therefore, but rather the rediscovery of an ancient custom that continues to be the rule in cultures other than our own. To eat with one's hands, in some Asian or African traditions, is still the common way of taking hold of food. Anything but new, the fashion of finger food is an echo of the past, a wish to retrieve the tactile contact with food, progressively strangled by "good manners." Which is why it is amusing to see alongside the "new" fashion the current drift toward bizarre accessories like the finger fork, a miniature fork to be worn on the finger for sampling among various bowls—a total contradiction in terms, because the point of the gesture is not to pierce the food but to feel it, physically, with one's own skin.

The missing cutlery

Human beings have everything needed for eating. Not only the ability to procure food for themselves, the capacity to choose plants and animals useful for sustenance, and the ingenuity to transform them into pleasurable dishes by means of fire and cooking practices. Humans also are endowed with a pair of fundamental instruments for eating: teeth, necessary for breaking up meat and vegetables; hands, for carrying them to the mouth. These instruments have for millennia been the ideal cutlery for humankind. Even in the recent past, the absence or rarity of forks in eating habits was simply a proof that the hands were adequate to the task (in Europe, barring local exceptions, the diffusion of the fork did not occur before the seventeenth and eighteenth centuries). More common was the use of the knife, not as a piece of individual cutlery but as a collective instrument, at the disposal of the guests for the first division of the dishes, after which all the guests served themselves—with their hands. If you look at the iconography from the Middle Ages and the early Modern Era, you see that the tables—even the highly symbolic ones that represent the Last Supper—set with cloths, glasses, plates, are notably lacking in individual cutlery: few knives, no forks.

On the other hand, the human body does not have a spoon. If teeth cut and hands grasp, liquid dishes cannot be consumed without an accessory, the complementary instrument of an object we call a spoon. Humans quickly learned how to make it, because liquid foods have been a constant presence in the daily diet since very ancient times. Crude bowls of wood or terra cotta, or more sophisticated cups of porcelain, glass, or precious metal have served to hold every kind of soup, pasta, broth, purée, along with the indispensable spoon. Spoons of every shape and material, poor and precious, plain or decorated, have for millennia accompanied, and continue to accompany, the evolution of eating customs. They are the most ancient and the most indispensable instrument devised by humans for eating.

The pot on the table

The tureen is an object that raises many questions for the historian. First among them is chronological: Is it possible to have had to wait until the eighteenth century for it to be invented? Is it possible that a society like the European one of the late Middle Ages, the Renaissance, the early Baroque—which knew how to embellish the table with every kind of art, enriching it with tableware of every shape and form, meticulously positioned according to architectural and geometric precisions, interspersed with limpid crystal and precious cutlery, marks of elegance and social distinction intended to amaze guests more than nourish them, to arouse admiration and envy within a behavioral framework of studied formality—a society of appearances, could not have found earlier the occasion to create objects as showy and theatrical as tureens, which made their first appearance in the eighteenth century?

A technical explanation can immediately be dismissed. Medieval and Renaissance ceramists were certainly not lacking the skill to produce an object as complex on the level of form and function as a tureen. More credible is a symbolic motivation. A tureen, intended to contain soup, evoked a centuries-old food of poverty. Porridge of cereals, legumes, and vegetables, flavored with a bit of lard or meat, was a dish with an unequivocal identity, a status symbol of the peasantry. Even broth was primarily associated with country folk and humble classes in whose kitchens (more often simple hearths in the middle of a room) the grates and spits, which in lordly houses held roasting meat, yielded to pots in which meat was boiled and reboiled to extract its last drop of flavor. One would then be tempted to think that soups, broths, and gruel were not appealing to the gentry, that such dishes were not worthy of appearing in a convivial setting. This hypothesis is denied by the evidence. Soups most definitely appeared on upper-class menus. One has only to leaf through the recipes of the great chefs of the sixteenth and seventeenth centuries (among them, Bartolomeo Scappi, cook for Pope Pius V, author of the most comprehensive treatise on the cuisine of the Italian Renaissance) to find all kinds of "poor" dishes, the gruel and soups of popular tradition, transformed by important enrichments, "exclusive" additions such as spices or sugar. Soups without soup tureens were therefore seen on the noble tables of the early Modern Era.

How were they served? Servants must have filled bowls before serving them to the guests. Or perhaps they went along the table offering the ladle directly from the pot. Or else, exceptionally, the pot was placed on the table. Evidence of this comes from an important cookbook of the end of the seventeenth century, *Lo Scalco alla moderna* (The Modern Carver) by Antonio Latini, published in two volumes between 1692 and 1694. One recipe is for *"minestra di foglie alla napolitana,"* salad soup in the Neapolitan style. It is one of those soups that drowns in a multitude of ingredients and flavors what we assume was the original simplicity of the peasant version: Chicken and beef, salted pig's tongue, salami, filet, pork belly, sausages, lard are the basic ingredients, to which were added squash, onions, eggs, bread, pine nuts, spices, and fragrant herbs, with the possible additions of lettuce, escarole, parmesan, mushrooms, and still more. Beyond the recipe, which is a good example of how rich and complex a "lordly" soup could become at the end of the seventeenth century, it is interesting to note the final remark of the author: "Many times," Latini writes, "I have had these soups brought to the table right in the pot," because this way "they are satisfying to the eye and [have] better flavor" and "can then be ladled into plates."

Here we are but a step away from the introduction of the tureen. The pot will continue to come to the table, but it will no longer be the metal receptacle just lifted from the kitchen stove; rather, a piece of gleaming multicolored porcelain, beautiful "to the eye" and capable of maintaining "better flavor."

First or second?

Eating habits are changing. We eat less and tend, above all, to deconstruct the meal into two distinct parts. Some dietitians as well as the ministry of health recommend cutting portions in half. It has not been determined how many people are observing this, but many are apparently replacing it with a similar rule in the results, if not in the method. Instead of the traditional meal *all'italiana,* which is still in practice in moderately priced restaurants, with its typical first course, main course, and dessert, now it is more common to choose either a first or a second course. This happens frequently in restaurants, but also, for many, at home: a first course (or a second) at lunch; a second (or a first) at dinner. For that reason I speak of the deconstruction the meal, as though it were two successive stages integrated one with the other.

These new customs signal a different relationship with food. After decades of overeating, a compensation for the hunger endured for centuries, we have by now become accustomed to abundance and are able to manage it better. But it must also be said that there was something strange, anomalous about the so-called meal *all'italiana*, decidedly in crisis today. In all European countries the structure of the typical meal consisted of three courses: a light "opening," a main dish, and a "finale" preferably sweet (dessert). This structure has infinite variations but is nonetheless characterized by a ternary rhythm, with a rising phase and a descending phase that frame the central dish, the protagonist of the menu, generally meat or fish, garnished with vegetables. In English this is the "main course," in French, more simply *"le plat,"* the dish. Why, then, does the so-called Italian tradition have not one but two protagonists? Why a "first" and a "second"?

I do not believe that this is at all "traditional." In the Middle Ages, when there was no dearth of meat, an Italian meal was similar to that of other European countries. Later, meat slowly disappeared from the diet of peasants and the urban poor. Pasta, which at first was a side dish for meat (or could replace it in periods of religious abstinence), ended up taking its place. The roles were reversed and it was meat, when there was any, that became the side dish as *ragù,* meat sauce. The same thing happened in other regions to rice and polenta. During the twentieth century, meat became accessible and returned to the menu, but the custom of a one-dish meal of pasta (or rice or polenta) had already taken root in daily use. It did not disappear, but took its place along with a meat dish. The structure of the menu doubled, the protagonists became two.

Two roosters in a chicken coop have a hard time living together. A "proper" menu requires one main dish, not two. Which is why we are witnessing a formal divorce, with rights of space, and time, to each party. The new customs seem to me a sign of rediscovered rationality, of a new order that recalls the old.

The wheel of food

In Chinese restaurants the table is generally round, and on the table is a smaller wheel, a revolving tray known as a "lazy Susan," on which many small serving dishes are placed. The diners, by turning the tray, stop it at the dish they want and serve themselves, filling their plate with the combination of dishes and flavors they prefer.

The purpose and meaning of this practice are numerous. More than anything else it emphasizes and amplifies the convivial, communal dimension of the meal. The sharing of serving dishes also expresses this idea visually, modifying the relationship between the diners and the meaning of being together at the table. This encourages conversation as well, in the form of opinions and suggestions regarding which foods to try: "Taste this too; it's good." The very shape of the table makes it the best possible for conversation. The circle is the one shape that does not allow for a head of the table; it equalizes places, eliminates hierarchies.

There is more. This system of serving food is derived from a culture, a "philosophy" of food that is rooted in an ancient scientific and dietary, as well as gastronomic, tradition. According to this tradition, it is unthinkable that all the diners eat the same thing, in the same order, and in the same amount. Because each organism is physiologically different from any other, each one has different needs and desires and adjusts his own meal to his own "nature." In Europe as well, dietary thinking (coming out of the medical tradition of ancient Greece) long adhered to this model. Until the Middle Ages and the early Modern Era, the modalities of table service were determined by the idea that each person has to compose his own menu freely by selecting from the table the foods he prefers. Not until the nineteenth century did service "à la Russe" become common in Europe, still practiced today, which presents all the diners with previously selected and generally identical dishes.

On the Chinese revolving tray, the simultaneous presence of various foods (meat, fish, vegetables, rice) and the systematic mixing of flavors (sweet, salty, spicy, sweet, and sour) go back to the same ancient precept. The idea that each individual should compose his own plate according to his own needs runs parallel to the idea that as a rule, a food is all the more suitable when it contains various substances and flavors. The balance of opposites, the co-presence of contrasts is fundamental to ancient Chinese philosophy—as it is to Indian, Persian, and Greek philosophies—traces of which are still seen in the way food is prepared and served.

To pour, to mix: when wine was made by the imbiber

Medieval wines were very different from what we drink today. They were weaker, did not keep well, and were particularly appreciated young and fresh. There are many suggestions by agronomists on how to limit the negative effects of eventual undesired aging. It is advised, for example, to add new wine and must to old wine to "rejuvenate" it. Only a few wines of particular esteem, classified as "sweet and strong" were capable of keeping over the years. They were drunk in small amounts or to celebrate special occasions, or for therapeutic purposes as tonics. In this category of wines, Madeira, also known in English as malmsey, and the so-called Greek wine were particularly renowned.

Other wines were drunk more liberally and on any occasion. They were, however, constantly corrected by the consumer. More than a product, as we understand wines today, they were perceived as a primary matter requiring subsequent treatment. Herbs, flowers, spices, fruit, honey were all added to them, considerably altering their original nature. Temperature was similarly altered. Wines were heated and chilled, even cooked and thickened by the heat.

Moreover, as in antiquity, wine was normally thinned with water. To put it another way, water was thinned with wine. For water was never drunk by itself, being hygienically unverifiable, as it still is in many countries. The habit of regularly drinking the two liquids together, taken for granted and almost required, explains why in ancient and medieval Latin, a single verb, *miscere*, to blend, indicates two actions as different as "to pour" and "to mix." Two actions, one word, or two actions perceived as simultaneous.

Color was also a matter of great concern. White wine was appreciated when very clear and pale, so that egg white was added to make it more luminous and transparent. During the last centuries of the Middle Ages "*chiaretto*," obtained in this way, was much in fashion on noble tables, indicative of finesse and exquisite gallantry. Red wine, on the other hand, generally less esteemed and considered more plebeian, was enjoyed very strong and deeply colored, and when it was not so, it was tinted with wild grapes or dark berries. All this fit perfectly with a culture, like that of the Middle Ages, that was deeply marked, even in the realm of gastronomy, by the idea of artifice and the "construction" of food—in this case of beverage—in its every aspect: flavor, color, consistency.

The ancient art of pairing wine with food

The idea that every food can be paired with the "right" wine is not new. Medieval treatises on dietetics discuss this amply and knowledgeably. These are dietetic—that is, medical—treatises, and this suggests the divergence of opinion regarding present-day parameters. Pairing is not generated by criteria of taste alone, which are somewhat arbitrary even though they are "scientific" in the classification of foods and beverages. This is not a proposal or a suggestion, but a rule. With certain foods, under certain conditions, one *must* drink certain wines.

Such prescriptions were based, as always, on the theory of the four conditions (cold, hot, dry, wet) that for more than two thousand years determined scientific thinking and daily practices. The achievement of equilibrium, the interaction of the temperaments, aimed at deterring excesses by combining and balancing the nature of foods, held for beverages as well. It is this cultural context that led to directions on which foods go together and how to pair food and drink, in particular wine, always with the goal of reaching an ideal point of balance.

What were the characteristics of wine? Beyond a few general indications, which usually classify it as hot and wet (and for that reason increasing moderation was recommended as one ages, in view of the fact that with time one becomes progressively colder and dryer), the problem remains unresolved because that heat and that wet are subject to varying degrees of intensity and a host of other variables that determine from one occasion to another *which* wine (who today would talk about wine in the singular?). Among the many kinds of wine, wrote Cesare Crivellati in 1550, "some are new, some old, some white, others red, some raw, others cooked, some transported, others not, some fragrant, others not, some from hilltops, others from valleys, some strong, others weak, some delicate, others coarse, some flavorful, others insipid" (*Treatise on the Use and Method of Administering Wine in Cases of Serious Illnesses*). These, as can be seen, are classifications in large part based on the idea of color, smell, flavor—characteristics directly perceptible to the drinker. Premodern dietary science was intimately related to the sensory, convinced as it was that the sensory, in first place flavor, constituted the key to the nature of a food, and the simplest, as well as the surest and most precise way of determining its quality and nutritive virtues.

As for the pairing of food and wine, the norms were incontrovertible and clear to all. Cold, wet foods, like fish, required strong, hot wines that corrected their coldness. This compensatory objective was the reason for recommending hot wines to accompany many fruits, generally classified as cold. Choices contrary to those of today originated from these principles that often (even if not always) preferred to pair foods and wines for their affinity rather than their for opposition: delicate with delicate, strong with strong. The difference between then and now is startling when we consider the pairing of wine with meat and fish: "The wine must be stronger with fish than with meat," wrote Maino de'Maineri, a Milanese doctor of the fourteenth century, in his well-known *Regimen sanitatis.*

How to taste wine (without making an ass of oneself)

Tasting wines to evaluate their quality, aroma and flavor is not an art invented by the sommeliers of today. Some seven hundred years ago, at the start of the fifteenth century, Pietro de' Crescenzi, the Bolognese author of an important treatise on agriculture (the most famous of the time), devoted to this topic discussions that can still be read with interest, even if they are part of a cultural context very different from our own. For example, in that culture, it was taken for granted that there were ties between alimentary products and lunar cycles, astral connections, the drift of winds, connections that have endured in the peasant tradition (as, for example, the influence of the moon at the time of bottling wine).

Crescenzi reports that the experts do not agree about the best time for a tasting. Some like to try wines when the boreal winds are blowing from the north, because then "they are immutable," not subject to change, and can thus be better evaluated. Others are of exactly the opposite opinion. They prefer tasting wines when a hot wind is blowing from the south, which "moves the wine more," and precisely for that reason allows its most intimate nature to be appreciated.

Another question raised by Crescenzi: Is it better to taste wine on an empty stomach or a full stomach? His opinion is clear: to understand a wine, one must not have eaten or drunk too much, or at least have thoroughly digested the meal. Nor should one be fasting (even though some, like Crescenzi's fellow citizens, thought otherwise). In any case, it is essential to avoid bitter things, "neither salad nor anything else that could affect the sense of taste."

There are also suggestions for protecting oneself against the skulduggery of wine sellers (here Crescenzi refers primarily to tavern keepers). Some, "wishing to fool the buyer," have on tap a new cask, well "scented with excellent aged wine," into which they put "the wine they wish to sell," to make it seem better. One must beware. One must also beware of even more conniving sellers who "offer walnuts and cheese" to those wishing to taste the wine before buying it, because walnuts and cheese "most assuredly falsify the sense of taste."

Crescenzi's remarks are repeated in the fifteenth century by another writer on agrarian subjects, Corniolo della Cornia of Perugia, who adds to the trickery of walnuts and cheese that of serving with wine "fennel, or other flavorful things." It is from this practice of medieval tavern keepers, who tried to fool the buyer by altering his sense of taste with fennel,[1] that the meaning we give still today to the verb *infinocchiare*, to make a fool of someone, may have been derived.

Cold drinks

The word may come from Arabic (*sharbah*; Turkish, *sharbat*) and it may be the Arabs who introduced sherbet[2] to the Europeans of Sicily and Spain as early as the Middle Ages. It was during the Renaissance that this took hold, no longer experimental but an established fashion. Italian gastronomy was then at the vanguard in Europe and it was in imitation of the Italian style that sherbet became popular in Europe.

From the very beginning gastronomy conflicted with dietetic concerns. When it comes to cooking, recipes, products, and preparations, medicine is always in the forefront, now as in the past,

---

[1] In Italian, *finocchio*.

[2] Initially, chilled fruit juice and sugar.

although even more so in the past. What I like to call "Galenic cooking" was a complex profession, typical of medieval and Renaissance culture, when the practices of eating and drinking were governed by specific references to medical science, based on the ancient findings of Hippocrates and Galen. The theory of hot and cold, dry and wet (the four fundamental conditions of everything in nature) persevered for more than two thousand years as the basis for judgment and choice regarding foods and drinks. That science viewed digestion as a process of cooking (likening the stomach to a kind of oven) and looked favorably on the "hot" elements in nature that could facilitate this function by providing heat. To this end, the generous use of spices was recommended for a very long time, and cold drinks were not advised: *"Nuoce molto l'acqua fresca quando è presa insieme all'esca"* (drinking cold water is very harmful when taken with food) was an aphorism of the Salerno school. It therefore took some effort to establish the legitimacy of cold drinks during or after ingesting food. Within this debate, reasons of taste and pleasure slowly found their way, justifying even dietetically the consumption of sherbet.

The decisive decades were those between the sixteenth and seventeenth centuries. Faced with a fashion that was holding on, a large number of doctors resisted. In the treatise *Regarding Hot Drinks in the Custom of the Ancient Romans*, published in 1593, Antonio Persio, a doctor, summons "history, the example of the ancients and of reason" as proof that "beverages heated on the fire are more pleasurable, and perhaps more flavorful, than the cold ones common today." Note the "perhaps" regarding flavor; he himself was evidently not entirely convinced. Four years later, the treatise by Nicola Masino appeared on the abuse of cold drinks (*De gelidi potu abusu*). Alessandro Peccana, in 1627, published *Regarding Drinking Cold Things, and Problems Concerning This Same Subject*. The debate raged throughout that century and into the next, with a growing propensity for "the benefits of iced drinks and the usefulness of drinking cold" (found in a medical treatise of 1716).

The desire to balance accounts, to justify gastronomic choices in terms of scientific rationality, slowly overturned the ancient convictions and left the way open to the art of sherbet-making. Cookbooks include it as an established craft. Antono Latini, in his *Modern Carver* (1692–94), devotes an entire chapter to the ways of making "different kinds of sherbets, or iced waters"), almost apologizing for stealing this craft from the specialists ("professors, butlers, cellarers") of this preparation. In 1775, the treatise *De' sorbetti,* by Philippo Baldini, appeared in Naples, the first work entirely devoted to this subject and based on the certainty, no longer open to discussion, that "iced drinks are a product of the most refined human intelligence and count as one of the results of a well-ordered society, that is, directed toward usefulness and pleasure."

TEN

"Identity" Declined in the Plural

Spaghetti with tomato sauce, or the other in us

When we talk about food, the subject of identity is often used in an openly reactionary way, to defend our own little garden, close the door to others, set an infrangible border between us and the "barbarians" who threaten us. The subject is very heated and its political, as well as its cultural, implications are very apparent. Because history is often called in as the guarantor of our identity, our "tradition," our "roots," it is the duty of the historian to point out that history teaches us exactly the opposite. It shows us that alimentary traditions never remain the same but change with time, becoming modified as they come into contact with other traditions. Identities, traditions invent themselves, in the literal sense of the word: they find themselves, they construct themselves. Origins, roots, by themselves explain nothing, They are necessary conditions but not adequate to explain the phenomena. Marc Bloch, the greatest historian of the twentieth century, liked to illustrate this idea with the example of the acorn and the oak tree. Without acorns there would be no oak tree, but not all acorns become oaks, because it is the type of terrain, climate, humidity that allows the acorn to develop its potential. These are the "historical" conditions. For example, nowhere was it written that in the Middle Ages, beginning with the encounter of Germanic culture and Latin culture, a new alimentary model and a new gastronomy that we call "European" would develop.

Another example is the so-called Mediterranean diet. Invented by American doctors in the 1950s and 1960s, this definition is equivocal for at least two reasons. It suggests the idea of a single diet and places history in the background, emphasizing the role of geographic space, as though this held (by determinism) the origins of history. It is, rather, history that created—among multiple and complex factors—not one, but many Mediterranean diets, which moreover underwent considerable change over time. So many elements in the alleged "Mediterranean diet" are not at all of Mediterranean origin, but come instead from exchanges with other cultures, other regions of the world. The Mediterranean cuisines of our time evoke the ancient world in the use of such products as bread, wine (which was banned from the Islamic Mediterranean table), olive oil, lamb, onion, garlic. Other flavors, other tastes have definitely undergone change; some have disappeared entirely. In ancient Greece and Rome sauces made of fermented fish (the most famous one was *garum*) were widely used. Today they can no longer be found in any Mediterranean cuisine, whereas they appear in the gastronomic traditions of southwest Asia (the Vietnamese *nuoc mam* is perhaps the best known). Similarly, the use of coriander, with its acrid-bitter flavor, disappeared, only to be found instead in Latin America (brought there by the Spanish), though it is coming back into use in Europe today as an "exotic" product. Conversely, other "Mediterranean" flavors have established themselves in the recent past. The eggplant and the artichoke were brought to Europe by the Arabs at the end of the Middle Ages; the tomato and beans (except for the Egyptian hyacinth bean) came from America in the Modern Era, along with corn and potatoes. So that Asia and America, along with Africa and Europe, have played an essential role in determining the characteristics of the alimentary system we call "Mediterranean."

Let us take a typical dish from Italian gastronomy, a dish intimately associated with Italian identity: spaghetti with tomato sauce. Its history has always seemed to me exemplary in the way it reflects the two notions of identity and roots, which in common parlance are often conflated, whereas they are completely distinct and diversely localized. Identities are values and models that define us here and now. Roots are the places and the impulses from which our identity took its origins, but do not necessarily belong to us. If we investigate the historical roots of spaghetti with tomato sauce we have to go back, on one side, to the Arab Middle East, whence the practice of making dry pasta in an elongated form came to Italy during the Middle Ages, and on the other to America, whence the tomato reached Europe in the Modern Era. The roots of our dish are therefore not at all European There is no doubt that they represent the Italian identity, because roots (origins) are not identity. Paradoxically, roots can be viewed as *the other in us*.

Pasta and the Italians: a single and multiple identity

Pasta means Italy. No other food identifies more effectively the many parts of Italian gastronomy and, in a way, unites them.

Italy has played a leading role in the history of establishing and disseminating the culture of pasta. Two traditions merged on Italian territory: the ancient Roman, of large fresh pasta, like lasagna, cooked in the dry heat of the oven with sauce spread only between each layer; and the Middle Eastern, developed primarily by Arabs, of long, thin pasta that could be dried more easily and stored longer (and precisely because it was dry, be cooked in water).

New techniques of preservation promoted the industrial production of pasta and its extraordinary commercial success, which placed the new product alongside the traditional, domestic one, presumed older, even if documents persist in giving us other information. The first pasta factory reported dates from the twelfth century in Trabìa, in the Arab part of Sicily, where, according to the chronicler Edrisi, "So much pasta is produced that it is exported all over, in Calabria and in other Muslim and Christian lands; and many shiploads are sent off." Later, others were built in Liguria ("Pasta of Genoa" remained for centuries a trusted gastronomic reference), and later still in northern Tuscany, Puglia, and Naples.

Pasta had been made at home for centuries. Fresh pasta, intended for domestic consumption, acquired a growing multiplicity of forms during the Middle Ages and Renaissance. Cookbooks describe lasagne, perforated macaroni, *corzetti*,[1] fettuccine, and all the filled forms of fresh pasta—tortelli, tortellini, and tortelletti, with cheese or meat—that by themselves constitute an important chapter in the history of Italian gastronomy.

Pasta seems made to order as a metaphor for the unity and variety of Italian alimentary styles. Pasta is singular, but it is declined in a hundred different forms, each intended for a particular purpose, a specific accompaniment to a particular sauce. Pasta is singular but it can also represent the sharing of a gastronomic culture that Italians knew how to exploit to the limit, making use of diverse traditions and turning them into a symbol of their identity. Pasta is also a way of expressing differences, of defining that identity in a thousand different ways, to demonstrate that a gastronomic identity can be at the same time single and multiple. This too is the fascinating secret of pasta.

Macaroni-eaters

In 1958 Emilio Sereni published a long essay, *Notes on the History of Food in the South of Italy: Neapolitans from Leaf-eaters to Macaroni-eaters.* It is a little masterpiece of methodology, a true

---

[1] A Genoese pasta, rarely found today outside of Genoa, stamped with the crest of a noble family and a cross.

classic that still has much to offer us. In particular, it teaches us that the history of food is a complex discipline containing a mixture of economics and culture, sociology and politics, the concrete and the imagined, and that all this combined to determine the "structures of taste," as it was termed by the French historian Jean-Louis Flandrin.

Structures is a fitting term because taste in food is not a gratuitous reality determined by personal whim but has it roots in specific historical realities. Sereni sets out to understand "when, how, and why" the taste for macaroni spread in Naples, to the point of justifying the appellation of "macaroni-eaters" by which Neapolitans were known as of the Middle Ages. Analyzing very closely a large number of documents, Sereni shows that until then this appellation had been applied not to Neapolitans but to Sicilians. This does not surprise the historian, because Sicily in the Middle Ages was the region of Italy where industrialized dry pasta first took hold. Other pasta factories started up later in Liguria. As a result, these two denominations, Sicilian and Ligurian, marked pasta recipes for centuries, for it was primarily those zones that produced commercial pasta.

In Naples, on the other hand, pasta was still regarded as a luxury in the sixteenth century, a special treat for special occasions. On lists of products, pasta was associated with sweets, and in years of famine, the manufacture of pasta was prohibited so as not to "waste" wheat. Then there was a radical change, which Sereni places around 1630. The market of Naples had been impoverished as a result of famine and the bad government of Spain, to which that part of the Italian peninsula then belonged. Meat, until then available even to the lower classes, became extremely scarce. Neapolitans—first called "leaf-eaters" because the "leaf" (cabbage) was their principal food, along with meat—were forced to create a new alimentary regimen for themselves. In the interim, new inventions had appeared (the wine press and the mechanical pasta maker) that lowered the price of pasta. Macaroni thus became the new food of Neapolitans.

Here, then, is how the Neapolitan taste for pasta was born, and how the epithet "macaroni-eater" migrated from Sicily to Naples. In the nineteenth century Italians as a nation came to be known by that term.

Emilio Sereni's research is exemplary because it demonstrates the connections between food and politics, food and economics, food and technology, food and culture.

Four pies

We are not talking about sweet pies, but about what was understood between the Middle Ages and the Renaissance as a savory pie, filled with meat, fish, eggs, cheese, vegetables, according to season and availability at the market, individual possibilities and tastes, traditions and local customs. In the Middle Ages the outer crust was preferred hard and was not eaten; later it was made edible as pie crust or puff pastry.

I often have occasion to talk about these pies when I discuss the theme of Italian cuisine and its regional variations, or rather its urban variations, because in Italy it is the cities, above all, that developed gastronomic culture using the resources of the countryside, reworking local skills and putting them into circulation through the network of local markets. This very network makes me think of a "national" culture that united the country long before it also achieved political unity (not until the mid-nineteenth century). From the standpoint of culture (we are talking about cuisine, thus culture), an Italian community existed—a minority but not insignificant—long before Italy. We can already recognize it in the cookbooks of the Middle Ages and the Renaissance, which reflect not local traditions but the intermixing of products and recipes that cut across the country in all directions.

Bartolomeo Scappi, that most celebrated chef of the Renaissance, and probably of all time, left in his cookbook of 1570 an enormous collection, almost an anthology of local recipes attributed to many

Italian cities, in many of which Scappi had worked himself: Milan, Venice, Bologna were the stages of his profession, which later ended in Rome at the papal court of Pius V, where he recorded his experiences in a monumental cookbook, modestly entitled *Opera,* works. What was Scappi's method? He assembled and compared different recipes, without postulating hierarchies or assigning priorities. All of them seemed equally interesting and worthy of mention. For the pies he proposed four types: as made in Milan, Bologna, Genoa, and Naples. The dish is more or less the same, expressing a largely shared culture. What distinguishes them are the ingredients, the kinds of meat, vegetables, and fats used (butter in Milan, olive oil in Genoa), the height and the form (the Neapolitan pie can be open rather than covered, incorporating the model of the pizza). As in many other cases, the multiplicity of varieties is democratically respected. Each recipe is in its own way "right and authentic." It would be senseless, Scappi seems to be telling us, to ask which is the best. Try them all, and then decide. Italy is big and its heritage belongs to everyone.

One product, one city: Bologna and mortadella

There are products that seem to represent and almost explicate the identity of a place, its history, its culture. If you say "oranges," you think of Sicily. You say "spaghetti" and think of Naples, "*mostarda*"[2] and think of Cremona. For this to occur—to epitomize in a gastronomic image the identity of a place—two conditions intimately connected must be present. The first is that the product must have, aside from its individuality, a great deal of quality. The second is that the territory where such a product was created must be capable of exporting its image throughout the marketplace. Only when a regional product is capable of making itself known outside the zone of production can it become an indicator of a particular

---

[2] Pickled fruit relish.

identity. This is a phenomenon that repeats itself regularly in history. A product is "typical" because it is known, sold, consumed elsewhere, or even within the zone of production, but by people (travelers, tourists) who come from outside it. Identity does not exist without exchange. Identity is defined and constructed *as a function* of an exchange that is simultaneously economic and cultural, the market and the skill, the merchandise and the experience.

Mortadella from Bologna fills all these requirements. To begin with, it starts out as a luxury product, desirable, expensive. The simplistic, vaguely popular image that it has acquired in recent times is not part of its history, which may be ancient but can only be traced with certainty to the early centuries of the Modern Era. Second, mortadella qualifies as an exportable product. From the very start, it can be found in many markets of Italy and Europe, as well as ("more than" would be the way to put it) on local tables. The singular trait of this sausage, a great invention of Bolognese gastronomy, is its innate talent of making itself known outside of its birthplace. The process of identification that associates mortadella with Bologna, and even transfers the name of the city to the product (which became "bologna" by antonomasia in Italy and abroad) comes from its extraordinary ability to penetrate commerce, which even exceeds the ingenuity of its inventors.

Who knows why mortadella comes from Bologna? Who knows why it is a cooked cold cut (or one that has to be cooked, in the case of a less known variant) in a country that prefers raw cold cuts (salami, prosciutto, etc)? Who knows why its contents are highly refined and secret (giving rise to improbable legends) in a country of traditional cold cuts that are simpler and often coarse? Who knows why its appearance and color make it eccentric compared with most Italian cold cuts, and more like the gastronomic culture north of the Alps? What comes to mind are the many kinds of *würstel* (frankfurters, knockwurst, bratwurst), and this comparison is not heretical. During the Middle Ages, which saw the incubation of Bolognese mortadella as an original product, very distinguishable from the large family of Italian cold cuts, Bologna had singularly close and frequent contacts with Germany, France, and the countries of Eastern Europe. I do not mean to suggest that mortadella is a big würstel, but merely to underscore the cultural, and thus gastronomic, relations that this city, more than others in Italy, maintained with Europe during those centuries because of the ancient and prestigious University of Bologna, which attracted students and professors from the entire continent.

The international nature of Bologna manifested itself not only in a highly evolved culture of hospitality, and the determination, which was also a political choice, to offer foreigners the best of its own cuisine (public notices of the sixteenth and seventeenth centuries express great concern that travelers and guests be properly fed in the inns and taverns of the city), but also in the uncommon initiative to collect suggestions and improvements from outside. Few were the cities where one could eat in the French or German style along with the local one, as attested by travelers going through Bologna in the seventeenth century.

If the interplay of markets and the reciprocal exchange of products, skills, and techniques were, ever since the Middle Ages, a constant factor in Italian gastronomy, developed and introduced particularly into the cities, Bologna was in a way an archetype, or at least a model, of this phenomenon. A center of commercial and cultural exchanges, opulent ("*grassa*") and learned ("*dotta*"), Bologna was always a crossroads of culinary inventions. The wealth of its gastronomic repertory allowed it to receive professors and students generously (the "*grassa*" made it possible for the "*dotta*" to exist), but at the same time, that repertory was enhanced by the multiplicity of cultures and experiences that intersected in the cities (it was thus the "*dotta*" that simulated the "*grassa*" and made it flourish). It is within this framework that we must place the advent of mortadella, which in the end became emblematic of the city. Whether it was indeed generated by this international intersection, we cannot know, but it assuredly served as a catalyst, contributing decisively to the exportation of the image of a powerful and victorious Bologna and her gastronomy. This play of mirrors alone allowed the ingenious invention of the artisans of Bologna to become the symbol of the city, to incarnate its meaning, its flavor, its aroma.

Pellegrino Artusi: Italian identity in the world

Pellegrino Artusi has been designated the father of nineteenth-century Italian cuisine. His *Scienza in cucina* (science in cooking), published in 1891 and enlarged in fourteen successive editions until the last in 1911, collected many local traditions, offering them to the middle-class citizen of a united Italy [since 1861] with the explicit intention of unifying the country through cooking (and succeeding, as plero Camporesi remarked, more effectively than Alessandro[3] Manzoni did with the Italian language). It was therefore an "Italian" mission that aimed at constructing a national gastronomic culture by bringing together the multifarious regional customs, with an eye on the trans-Appenine axis between Romagna and Tuscany, the area Artusi knew best since he was born in the one (Forlimpopoli), and lived in the other (Florence).

Artusi's cookbook, an astonishing and unexpected publishing success (and still today one of the best-selling books in all of Italian literature), was for generations the first and only cookbook of many families, the one that was given to brides as a wedding present, that sat in the kitchen among pots and pans, that emigrants took with them wherever they went. Recently, translations have also appeared, but with different criteria. Along with complete versions in English, Dutch, and Spanish, a German translation, in consultation with five contemporary chefs, selected some 200 recipes out of 790 and adapted them to the tastes of today.

But here is the problem: Can *Scienza in cucina*, a book that has had a life of more than a century, be revived today as just a cookbook? Or does it not represent instead a historical text, meaningful

---

[3] His novel, *Promessi sposi* (The Betrothed) of 1827 became symbolic of Italian nationhood.

primarily for its reconstruction of an era, a civilization that is no longer close to us? Italians, above all those of certain regions in the center-north, see in Artusi's book the roots of their own culture and read it on more than one level and in different ways: as a current text from which to glean technical and operational advice, and at the same time as a document of history, useful for reconstructing changes in consumption, customs, and tastes. This duality seems meaningful for non-Italian readers as well. The German publisher, with his arbitrary manipulation of the text, had a huge success (more than 100,000 copies sold); but in tiny Holland, some twenty thousand people bought the unabridged and "philological" Artusi, edited meticulously to the last linguistic detail as if it were a literary text. Wherever one turns, Artusi continues to be sold, and now not only in Italy.

Polenta and couscous (with an unexpected variant)

Certain foods have an identity powerful enough to become the symbol of a people, a community, a place. "Yes to polenta, no to couscous," read a poster raised some time ago in a city of the Veneto by a demonstrator who declared his political adherence by wearing a huge green kerchief around his neck.[4] "More couscous, less polenta" replied another poster held by another demonstrator with graying black hair, evidently of North African origin. This thrust and parry used polenta and couscous as symbols of a cultural identity, banners in a battle to be fought for the affirmation of the self against the other.

To identify a human group by the food that characterizes it is an ancient practice. In some cases this can stand as a proud representation of oneself (as when the ancient Greeks defined themselves as "bread-eaters," contrasting their agricultural civilization with the pre-civilized "barbarian" hunters). More commonly, these definitions arise externally (it is the *others*, from outside, who define our alimentary identity) and contain for the most part a negative

---

[4] Emblematic of a rightist anti-immigrant party in northern Italy.

prejudice. Appellations like "turnip-eaters" or "cat-eaters," historically attributed to this or that city, do not describe or evaluate eating habits but rather mock them and deride them. It was with disparagement that nineteenth-century Italian emigrants were called "macaroni-eaters" or just plain "macaroni," totally identifying the food with those who eat it. ("*Macaroni*" for the French were those Italian immigrants from across the Alps.) But the "macaroni-eaters" did not take long to turn the epithet around, vindicating the consumption of pasta as an integral part of their identity. Even the appellation "polenta-eater" started out derisively, but today, as we have just seen, it can be a proud sign of identity. The same happened with North African couscous.

Our attitude toward the food we eat, and that of others, reflects the way we view differences. Couscous and polenta can be wielded like a weapon, signifying an irremediable difference. Or they can be offered and shared, helping others to understand their meaning, convivial and social as well as gastronomic (as was admirably demonstrated by the film *Cous Cous* by Abdellatif Kechiche, which won an award at the Venice festival in 2007). They can even become a means of integration—for example, by including couscous in school menus as an alternative to pasta or polenta, to encourage familiarity with other eating habits (a practice fairly common today after pilot experiments some twenty years ago). And one might even discover the existence of an "impossible" dish that combines couscous and tortellini, like the one a Moroccan child in a school in Emilia declared he had eaten at home, prepared by his mother, which he thought was very good.

Is McDonald's compatible with local identities?

Food is a fundamental instrument of cultural identity. The best recipe is always mama's, because in it (in mama and everything she represents) one finds, or chooses to find, the roots of one's personal identity. But then, when mama's food comes up against

McDonald's, do we find ourselves faced with a conflict between the affirmation and the annulment of identity? Between identity and non-identity?

Not at all. If the global village is not the invention of the sociologist Marshall McLuhan but is a reality of our daily life, even that identity belongs to us. The citizen of Imola (who recognizes himself in the food of his city and his countryside) is also a citizen of Romagna, of Italy, of Europe. Each one of these identities—all changeable, all in construction—wants its own alimentary symbols. The global village has McDonald's, identical everywhere, reassuring, maternal (that capital M, as round as a breast). To think of a hamburger as non-culture, non-identity is a serious error of perspective. On the symbolic level, the hamburger holds a much greater cultural density than would appear at first glance.

Moreover, a hamburger is never equal to itself. It is accompanied everywhere by market studies that speak not only the language of numbers but also (in second place, one hopes) that of tastes and traditions. The sauce is not the same everywhere. The balance of sweet and salty varies from country to country. The uniformity of taste does not exclude variants, and this means that not even the hamburger can disregard local identities. These days McDonald's is obliged to go so far as to cohabit with vegetarian dishes. Perhaps this indicates that McDonald's cooking and home cooking can live together. I would go farther: The very diffusion of global alimentary models, such as McDonald's and its competitors, has paradoxically stimulated the search for diversity, the reconstruction of more or less invented roots, the rediscovery of "local" traditions. The body politic has developed a powerful antidote to the threat of cultural homogeneity. To network local cultures, spread them, make them known, share them, is the positive response to this threat, by using the global village as a place of exchange rather than homogenization, globalizing gastronomic and cultural biodiversity.

INDEX

Abelard, Pierre, 132
abstinence, 48, 49, 104–9, 131–33; and
    new inventions, 132–33
Agrarian Practice (Battara), 102
agriculture: and environment, 12, 25; *vs.*
    hunting, 12–13, 167
Aldobrandino of Siena, 132
Aldrovandi, Ulisse, 24, 57, 65
America: barbecuing in, 125–26; choco-
    late in, 90–91; fruit from, 33; as land
    of plenty, 75–77; and Mediterranean
    diet, 61; pigs in, 47; plants from, 44,
    46, 61, 114, 158; and spices, 88; sugar
    in, 82
Ammiano Marcellino, 38
Annibale II Bentivoglio, 116
Anthimus, 39
Apologia of Abbot William (Saint Ber-
    nard), 110
Appert, Nicolas, 93
Arabs: bread of, 8; and eggplant, 24,
    61; and Mediterranean, 60–61; and
    pasta, 61, 159; and sugar, 61, 82, 90;
    and wine, 158
Aristotle, x, 88, 94, 116; and colors, 115;
    on flavors, 79, 80, 81; on men as
    social animals, 137
artichokes, 61, 158
artifice, 3, 116–17; color as, 112; compote
    as, 118, 119; confections as, 120; of

fast food, 140; and grinding, 59; and
    health, 96; and wine, 150–51
Artusi, Pellegrino, 5, 23, 25, 50, 131; on
    frittata, 51, 52; and Italian identity,
    166–67; on pasta, 129–30
arugula (rucola), 126–27
Atheneus, 13

Baldini, Philippo, 156
barbecuing, 123–26
barley, 7, 14, 15, 16, 17, 71, 73
Barnard, abbot of Clairvaux, 48
Battarra, Giovanni, 22, 46, 75, 102
beauty, 81, 116, 121–22
beer, 16–18
Benedict, Saint, 67, 108
Bernard of Clairvaux, Saint, 110
Bertin, Saint, 73
Bible, 12–13, 36, 100
bitterness, 84–85
Bloch, Marc, 157
Boccaccio, Giovanni, 43, 76
Bologna, 27, 42, 100, 116, 163; bread of,
    5, 130; sausages of, 53, 163–66
Bonnefons, Nicolas de, 20
bread, 2–8; and beer, 16–17; of Bologna,
    5, 130; chestnuts as, 25; as divider,
    6–8; festive, 5–6; made of earth,
    72–74; potato, 75, 102; and religion,
    4–5, 7–8; substitutes for, 73, 74, 75

breakfast, 134–35
Brecht, Bertolt, 131
Breughel, Pieter, 113, 131
Brillat-Savarin, Anthelme, 121
broth, 9, 43, 44–46, 76, 91, 146; and
    pasta, 45, 129, 130. *See also* soup
butter, 5, 76, 136, 163; frying with, 23, 47,
    50, 51–52; and pasta, 11, 44, 114, 143;
    in sauces, 86, 88

Caesar, Julius, 101
Camporesi, Piero, 130, 166
canning, 92–93. *See also* preservation
capons, 43, 76, 77, 104, 129, 130
cappelletti: and broth, 45; on Christmas,
    129–30; fillings of, 42–43
cardoons, 67–68
Carnival, 131–32
carrots, 115–16, 118
Carrù, fat bull of, 101, 102
Cassiano, Giovanni, 137
Cassiodoro, 67
castagnacci (baked product made of
    chestnut flour), 26
Castelvetro, Emilian Giacomo, 25, 26,
    39, 115
Cato, 36
Celano, Tommaso da, 128
Charlemagne, 101, 104
cheese, 42, 44; and fruit, 98; and monks,
    48, 109; and preservation, 70, 99; in
    utopias, 43, 76–77; and wine, 154
chestnuts, 25–27, 73
Chevreul, Michel, 80
chicken. *See* poultry
Chinese cooking: and law of opposites,
    97; senses in, 121, 144; and serving
    practices, 149, 150; sourness in, 86;
    and vegetarianism, 56
chocolate, 85, 90–92, 113, 134
Chrétien de Troyes, 38–39
Christianity, 48, 50, 61; and abstinence,
    131, 132; and bread, 7–8; and holi-
    days, 127, 133; and pleasure, 106–9;
    and raw *vs.* cooked, 38. *See also*
    Bible; monks
Christina, Queen of Sweden, 32
Christmas, 5–6, 82, 127–30

Cicero, 52
Cirio, 93
coffee, 85, 91
cold, as preservative, 93
cold drinks, 154–56
Colombano, abbot of Bobbio, 21
colors, 112–16; and beauty, 116; of car-
    rots, 115–16; in compotes, 118; of
    sauces, 113–14; and wine, 151, 152
Columella, 36
companatico (that which goes with
    bread), 4
compotes, 117–19
confections, 119–21
conviviality, xi, 9, 123–42; and barbecu-
    ing, 123–26; and fast food, 141–42;
    and holidays, 82, 102, 127–30; and
    identity, 168; and serving practices,
    146, 149
coriander, 118, 158
corn: from America, 46, 61, 158; and
    malnutrition, 22, 72
Corniolo della Cornia, 115, 116, 154
Country Wedding, A (painting;
    Breughel), 113
couscous, 167–68
Cous Cous (film), 168
Crescenzi, Pietro de', 153–54
Crialese, Emanuele, 75
Crisippus, 52
Crivellati, Cesare, 152
Croce, Giulio Cesare, 103, 130
cucumbers, 34
culture, 2, 72–74; of bread, 3, 4; and
    breakfast, 134–35; and hunger,
    73–74; and identity, 157, 158, 160; of
    Middle Ages, 157–58; and snacks,
    137; and taste, 41; and wild plants, 67
cutlery, 143–45

Damiani, Pier, 109–10
De anima (Aristotle), 115
De gelidi potu abusu (Masino), 155
de'Maineri, Maino, 94, 153
De' sorbetti (Baldini), 156
desserts, 84, 90, 113, 130; and serving
    practices, 147–48. *See also* confec-
    tions

Diocletian, 100
Dioscorides, 34
diversity: in cooking, 40, 61; cultural, 60–61, 71, 85; in flavors, 83; of fruits, 68, 69; geographic, 41–43; and hunger, 71–72; of taste, 86
dolceforte, 92
Durand, 93
Durante, Castore, 26
Durante da Gualdo, Castor, 115

Easter, 133–34
Edrisi, 160
eggplant (*melanzana*; aubergine), 23–25; and Arabs, 24, 61; grilling of, 123, 124; and Mediterranean diet, 158
eggs, 47–49, 51, 52; Easter, 133–34
Egypt, 3, 14, 16, 17, 99
Emilia-Romagna region, 42
environment: and agriculture, 12, 25; and beauty, 121; and fast food, 142; and health, 98; and regional cuisine, 41, 42; and vegetarianism, 56
Erardo, Bishop, 106
Etruscans, 100

fast food, 46, 105, 140; and conviviality, 141–42
fat: *vs.* lean, 132–33; and Lent, 49; and meat, 101–2; positive views of, 100–101
Felici, Costanzo, 34, 36; on salads, 24, 39, 57, 58, 115; on sweetness, 82; and wild plants, 65–66, 68
fennel, 67–68
Feuerbach, Ludwig, 1–2
Fick, Adolf, 80
figs, 35–37
finger food, 143, 144
Flandrin, Jean-Louis, 4, 84, 103, 161
flavors, 78–93; in beer, 17; and colors, 115, 116; and form, 11; number of, 79–81; of pasta, 10–11; smoky, 88–90; and taste, 78–79, 80; and wine, 152
"Flavors of the Mediterranean" (colloquium; Barcelona, 2004), 60
forks, 143–44, 145

four conditions (hot, cold, dry, wet), theory of, 94–95, 151–53, 155. *See also* Galenical medicine; opposites, law of
Francis, Saint, 128–29
French cuisine, 98, 165
French language, 10
French Revolution, 9
frittata, 51–52
fritters, 49–51
Frugoli, Antonio, 24
fruit: citrus, 26, 61; in compotes, 118; cultivation of, 29, 30, 32–33; forgotten, 68–69; and monthly diets, 99; and salt, 97, 98; and social divisions, 27–37; taste of, 74; and wine, 29–30, 31, 35, 37
frying: of fritters, 49–51; of potatoes, 46–47
fusion cuisine, 60

Galenical medicine, 29, 31, 36–37, 155. *See also* four conditions; opposites, law of
Gallo, Agostino, 26
garlic, 114, 126; sauces with, 44, 76; and social divisions, 18–19, 97
garum (fermented-fish sauce), 158
Genoa, 160, 163
Gerard of Cambrai, 138
German cuisine, 45, 158, 165
German language, 1–2, 17
Ghiradacci, Cherubino, 116
Ghisilieri, Lippo, 27–28
Girolamo, Saint, 107
Glaber, Raoul, 72
globalization: and fast food, 140; *vs.* regional cuisine, 140–41, 169; and seasonality, 33, 141
gluttony, 109–11, 130
gnocchi, 43–44, 47
Goethe, Johann Wolfgang von, 127–28
grains: and beer, 17; diversity of, 71; inferior, 7, 14, 15–16; substitutes for, 73. *See also* spelt
Greece, ancient: beauty in, 121–22; and bread, 2, 6–7; foods in, 13, 14, 36; and identity, 167; law of opposites

Greece (*continued*)
in, 97; and raw *vs.* cooked, 38; sauces in, 158; and seasons, 99; serving practices in, 150
Gregory of Tours, 73
grinding, 58–60
Guida gastronomica d'Italia (Gastronomic Guide of Italy), 5

Hahn, 93
health: and breakfast, 135; and cold, 154–55; and color, 116; and confections, 120; and fat, 102; and law of opposites, 96–97; and monks, 105; of peasants, 102–3; and pleasure, 94–111, 155; and serving practices, 147, 149; and snacks, 136; and social divisions, 102–4; and wine, 110, 151–53. *See also* Galenical medicine
Herodotus, 99
Hippocrates, 29, 36, 96, 97, 98, 155. *See also* Galenical medicine
holidays, 4, 82, 102, 127–30. *See also* Christmas; Easter
home cooking, 40, 61–62; and broth, 45, 46; *vs.* McDonald's, 169
honey, 6, 36, 82, 83
hops, 17
humors, 31, 37, 99. *See also* Galenical medicine
hunger, 65–77, 100, 130, 148; and culture, 73–74; and preservation, 69–71; and utopias, 75–77
hunting, 12–13, 124, 125, 167

Ibri al Awwam, 74
identity, 157–69; and conviviality, 168; and culture, 157, 158, 160; Italian, 166–67, 168; and pasta, 159–60; and regional cuisine, 163–66, 168–69
Ikeda, Kikunae, 80
Indian cuisine, 86, 97, 150
Instruction pour les jardins fruitiers et potagers (Quintinie), 29, 30
Ireland, 22–23, 72
Italian cuisine: compotes in, 118; and identity, 166–67, 168; law of opposites in, 98; monoculture in, 72;

pasta in, 10, 159–60, 168; raw vegetables in, 39, 57; regional, 160–66; sausages in, 53–54; tastes in, 41–43, 84; tomato sauce in, 113–14, 159
Italian language, 10, 13, 166

Japan, 50
Jews, 24–25
Judaism, 7, 133–34

Kechiche, Abdellatif, 168
Kim Jong-il, 74–75
kitchen, 63–64; *vs.* barbecuing, 124–25, 126; and pharmacy, 96–97

la Cruz, Sister Juana Inès de, x
lamb, 41, 42, 128, 134, 158
Lando, Ortensio, 53, 130
Land of Bengodi, 43, 44, 76
Land of Cockaigne, 70, 76, 127
La Rocca, Orazio, 142
L'arte di ben cucinare (The art of good cooking; Stefani), 32
Latini, Antonio, 114, 147, 156
Le Goff, Jacques, 68
Lent, 49, 50, 102; *vs.* Carnival, 131–32; and new inventions, 132–33
lentils, 12–13, 59
Le Pays de l'épautre (The Land of Spelt; bakery), 15, 16
Lévi-Strauss, Claude, 38
Liber de coquina, 21, 59
Libro de arte coquinaria (Book on the art of cooking; Martino), 51
Liebig, Justus von, 46
Liguria, 160, 161
Linnaeus, 80, 90
liqueurs, herbal, 84–85
Lorenzetti, Ambrogio, 55
Lo Scalco alla moderna (The modern carver; Latini), 147, 156
Louis XIV, 20, 21, 29, 33
Lupicino, Abbot, 107
Lusitano, Amato, 35

macaroni, 11, 43–44, 76
macaroni-eaters, 160–62, 168
Maintenon, Madame de, 20

Malaterra, Goffredo, 73
Manzoni, Alessandro, 27, 166
Marchesi, Gualtiero, 40, 113
Martino, Maestro, 20–21, 48, 50, 51–52
marzipan, 32, 53
Masino, Nicola, 155
Massonio, Salvatore, 34, 39
Mattioli, Pietro Andrea, 24
Mayas, 90
McCain, John, 125–26
McDonald's, 142, 168–69
McLuhan, Marshall, 169
meat: abstinence from, 48, 49, 108, 131,
    132; as artifice, 58, 59, 117; and fat,
    100, 101–2; grilling of, 123–26; and
    history, 41–42; on holidays, 127–28;
    in pies, 162–63; preservation of,
    70, 89; raw *vs.* cooked, 38–39; and
    serving practices, 144, 148, 153;
    and social divisions, 8–9, 13, 146,
    161; substitutes for, 56, 132–33; and
    sweetness, 90; and *umami*, 80. *See
    also* lamb; poultry; sausages
meatballs, ix, 9
Mediterranean diet, 60–61, 158
melons, 30–32
merenda ("snack"), 135–37
Mesopotamia, 3, 14, 16, 36
Messedaglia, Luigi, 43
Messisbugo, Cristoforo, 43, 88
Middle Ages: beauty in, 112, 118–19,
    120; beer in, 16, 17; bread in, 3, 6, 7;
    Carnival in, 131; culture of, 157–58;
    eggs in, 48, 49; fat in, 100, 133;
    flavors in, 11, 79, 80, 81, 82, 83, 86,
    87–88; fruits in, 29, 33, 37; grains
    in, 14, 15, 71; hunger in, 72; identity
    in, 161, 162, 164; meat in, 132; and
    Mediterranean, 60; monks in, 108;
    monthly diets in, 98–99; mortar
    in, 58; pasta in, 43, 160; pigs in, 54,
    55; preservation in, 89; and raw *vs.*
    cooked, 38; serving practices in, 145,
    148; sherbet in, 154; sign language in,
    137–39; social divisions in, 25, 103;
    vegetables in, 23, 24, 115; wine in,
    110–11, 151
millet, 7, 14, 15, 46, 71, 73, 82

minestra, 9
Modern Carver (*Lo Scalco alla mod-
    erna*; Latini), 147, 156
monks, 7, 48, 67, 105; abstinence of,
    104–9; and confections, 119–20; oral
    traditions of, 108–9; and pleasure,
    48, 108–11; sign language of, 137–39
monoculture, 71–72
monthly diets, 98–99
Moralia (Plutarch), 137
mortar and pestle, 58–60
Moulin, Léo, 109
names: of beer, 17–18; of bread, 5; of
    pasta, 10; plants without, 65–66

Naples, 59, 114, 127, 128, 147, 156, 163;
    macaroni in, 160–62
Nolfi, Vincenzo, 144
North Korea, 74–75
Nostradamus, 119
*Notes on the History of Food in the
    South of Italy* (Sereni), 160–62
Novellino, 24, 89
nuoc mam (fermented-fish sauce), 158
Nuovomondo (film), 75–76

oats, 7, 15, 71
Obama, Barack, 126–27
Obama, Michelle, 127
Odo, abbot of Cluny, 18
oil: *vs.* fat, 132; frying in, 23, 24, 47,
    49–50, 51; olive, 50, 54, 158, 163; as
    preservative, 54, 70, 92; and salads,
    58; in sauces, 86
olives, 47
On Safe Pleasure and Good Health
    (Platina), 37
On the Perfect Formation of a Monk
    (Damiani), 109
Opera (Works; Scappi), 163
opposites, law of, 94–97, 98, 150. *See
    also* four conditions; Galenical
    medicine
oral tradition: and home cooking, 62;
    and hunger, 65, 73; of monks, 108–9
orange juice, 26

Padella, Zuco, 27–28

panettone, 2, 5
Parmentier, Antoine, 46, 102
pasta, 9–11, 43–44; and Arabs, 61, 159; and broth, 45, 129, 130; and butter, 11, 44, 114, 143; commercial, 159–60, 161; filled, 42–43; in Italian cuisine, 10, 159–60, 168; Korean, 75; and Lent, 133; and serving practices, 148; and tomato sauce, 44, 113–14, 159. *See also particular types*
Pastore, Abbot, 106
Paul, Saint, 110
Paul II, Pope, 30–31
Paul the Deacon, 38
peaches, 27–28
pears, 29–30
peas, 19–21
Peccana, Alessandro, 155
pellagra, 22
peppers, 61; hot, 80, 87, 88
Persio, Antonio, 155
Peru, 21
pies, savory, 162–63
pigs, 41, 47; ancient breeds of, 54–55; and sausage, 52–53
Pior, Abbot, 106, 107
plants: from America, 44, 46, 61, 114, 158; wild, 65–68, 73; without names, 65–66
Platina (Bartolomeo Sacchi), 31, 35, 37, 48, 49, 82
pleasure, 23, 44, 53; and conviviality, 124, 128; and health, 94–111, 155; and hunger, 69, 71, 90; and monks, 48, 108–11; and preservation, 90; right to, 74–75; and the senses, 107, 144; as sin, 105–7; and social divisions, 16, 29, 75; and sweetness, 81–82
Pliny the Elder, 14, 36
Plutarch, 101, 137
Poem of Gilgamesh, 2
polenta, 7, 8, 22, 25, 43, 46; and identity, 167–68; and serving practices, 148
Pontremoli, Nicodemo di, 30
pork, 41–42. *See also* pigs; sausages
Portinari, Folco, 75
potatoes: from America, 44, 61; in bread, 75, 102; fried, 46–47; and

gnocchi, 44, 47; in Ireland, 22–23, 72; and Mediterranean diet, 158; and social divisions, 21–23
poultry, 26, 104–5, 128, 129, 130, 131
preservation, 39, 70, 99; *vs.* fresh foods, 92–93; and hunger, 69–71; in oil, 54, 70, 92; and pasta, 159; with smoke, 89–90
Procopius, 38
Prometheus, 38
Protestantism, 141

Quintinie, Jean-Baptiste de la, 29, 30, 33

Rabelais, François, 48, 130
Rashidy, Reza, 85
raw *vs.* cooked, 38–39
recipes: codification of, 40–41; and prescriptions, 96
refrigeration, 93
Regarding Drinking Cold things, and Problems Concerning This Same Subject (Peccana), 155
Regarding Hot Drinks in the Custom of the Ancient Romans (Persio), 155
Regimen sanitatis (de'Maineri), 153
regimina mensium (monthly regimen), 98–99
regional cuisine: and cultural identity, 163–66, 168–69; *vs.* globalization, 140–41, 169; in Italy, 160–66; *vs.* McDonald's, 168–69
Renaissance: beauty in, 112, 119, 120; chocolate in, 92; and fat, 101; flavors in, 78, 82, 83; mortar in, 58; pasta in, 43, 160; pies in, 162; poultry in, 104–5; sherbet in, 154
rice, 14, 45, 61, 148, 150; and color, 112, 113, 129
ricetta (recipe, prescription), 96
Romagna, 14, 42, 63, 166, 169; cappelletti of, 129–30
Rome, ancient, 36, 60, 159; breads in, 7, 13, 14; and European culture, 158; flavors in, 79, 86; and raw *vs.* cooked, 38
Rousseau, Jean-Jacques, 39
rucola (arugula), 126–27

rye, 7, 14, 15, 71, 73

Sabadino degli Arienti, 18, 19, 27
Sacchi, Bartolomeo. *See* Platina
saffron, 59, 112–13, 118
salads: ingredients of, 57–58, 86; of
    Obama, 126–27; and wild plants,
    65–66; and wine, 153
Salani, Massimo, 141
Salerno school, 30, 81, 87, 98, 155
salt, 57–58, 83–84, 92, 97, 98
sauces: colors of, 113–14; fermented-
    fish, 158; garlic, 44, 76; and grinding,
    58–59; and law of opposites, 96;
    sourness in, 86
sausages, 13, 52–54, 76, 89, 143, 147;
    and conviviality, 127, 132, 134;
    mortadella, 163–66; names for, 53;
    vegetable, 56
Scappi, Bartolomeo, 23, 40, 43, 54, 60,
    146; on kitchen, 63; and regional
    cuisines, 162–63
Scienza in cucina (Science in the
    kitchen; Artusi), 5, 23, 25, 50, 166–67
seasonality, 121; *vs.* globalization, 33, 141;
    and monthly diets, 98–99
senses, 78–79, 121, 144, 152. *See also*
    taste
Sereni, Emilio, 160–62
serving practices, 143–56; and convivial-
    ity, 146, 149; and cutlery, 143–45; for
    drinks, 150–56; for meat, 144, 148,
    153; for soup, 145–47
Shakespeare, William, 101
sheep, 41, 42. *See also* lamb
sherbet, 154, 156
Sicily, 24, 41, 53, 75, 159, 163; Arabs in,
    60, 154; pasta in, 161–62
Sigalini, Domenico, 142
sign language, monastic, 137–39
Sisoe (hermit), 106
slow food, 75, 105–7
smokiness, 88–90
snacks (*merendina*), 84, 135–37
social divisions, 12–37; and bread, 6–8;
    and chocolate, 90–91; and eggplant,
    23–25; and fat, 101, 102; and fruit,
    27–37; and garlic, 18–19, 97; and

health, 102–4; on holidays, 127–28,
    129; and kitchen, 63–64; and meat,
    8–9, 13, 146, 161; and pleasure, 16,
    29, 75; and potatoes, 21–23; and
    regionalism, 140; and soup, 146,
    147; and spices, 88, 97, 119, 120; and
    sugar, 83, 90, 120; and sweetness, 82,
    83; and wheat, 7, 14, 15
soup, 7, 14, 21, 59; in Bible, 12–13; and
    monks, 108, 109; and solidarity, 8–9;
    tureens for, 145–47. *See also* broth
soupe populaire, 9
sourness, 85–87, 115
Spain, 114
Spanish language, 17
spelt (*farro*), 7, 13–16, 46, 71, 73
spices, 87–88, 146, 155; and social divi-
    sions, 88, 97, 119, 120
Spoleto, duke of, 104
spoons, 145
Stefani, Barolomeo, 32, 33
strawberries, 32–34
sugar, 6, 32, 36, 146; and Arabs, 61, 82,
    90; and chocolate, 90; and health,
    120; and preservation, 92; and social
    divisions, 83, 90, 120
Sumeria, 2–3
Summa de saporibus, 79
sweetness, 81–83, 84; in chocolate,
    90–92; and figs, 35–37; and fruit,
    31, 32; and Mediterranean diet, 61;
    and saltiness, 83–84; and serving
    practices, 148; and social divisions,
    82, 83; and sourness,
    86

Tacitus, 17, 38
Tacuina sanitatis, 24
Tacuinum sanitatis (Platina), 48
Tanara, Vincenzo, 5, 24, 26, 55
Taoism, 97
taste: of broth, 45; diversity of, 86;
    and flavor, 78–79, 80; of fruit, 74;
    geography of, 41–43, 140; limita-
    tions of, 114; and pleasure, 107, 144;
    and preservation, 90; and smell, 121;
    structures of, 161; sweet-salty, 83–84
tempura, 50

teriaca (universal antidote), 97
tofu, 56
tomatoes, 24, 61; and color, 112; grilling of, 123, 124; and Mediterranean diet, 158; and pasta, 44, 113–14, 159
tortellini, 42–43, 45
traveling, eating while, 139–41
Treatise on the Use and Method of Administering Wine in Cases of Serious Illnesses (Crivellati), 152
Turkey, 98
Tuscany, 35, 50, 160, 166

umami, 80
utopias: and hunger, 75–77; Land of Bengodi, 43, 44, 76; Land of Cockaigne, 70, 76, 127

vegetables: canned, 92–93; and fat *vs.* lean, 132–33; raw, 39, 57–58; and social status, 20

vegetarian cooking, 56–57, 108–9
Vietnam, 97, 158
vinegar: and chocolate, 91; in compotes, 118; and preservation, 70, 92; on salads, 57–58, 86
vitamins, 39, 95

watermelons, 34–35, 97, 98
wheat, 10, 16; and social divisions, 7, 14, 15; *vs.* spelt, 7, 13–14. *See also* bread
Widerard (monk), 119
wine, 3, 150–54; appreciation of, 110–11; and beer, 16; and food, 151–53; and fruit, 29–30, 31, 35, 37; and Mediterranean diet, 158; mixing of, 150–51; tasting, 153–54
women, 3, 65–66, 124–25

Yvain, the Knight with the Lion (Chrétien de Troyes), 38–39

Zacchia, Paolo, 10